Sorting through Worldviews

"If it is difficult for you to talk with someone about Jesus, this book is for you. In it, you will find creative, interesting, and simple ways to converse with anyone without being confrontational."

—**RAY BEESON**
Founder, Overcomers Ministries

"Rick Kline masterfully and uniquely responds to the hard questions, criticisms, and skepticisms raised against the Christian faith by wrapping powerful logic in warm and respectful conversation . . . The combination of the insights in this single book makes *Sorting through Worldviews* a work of profound value and use, and thus highly recommended."

—**MARK PATTERSON**
Director, Flourish Institute: Graduate School of Ministry

"Kline's abilities to listen deeply, process thoroughly, and respond lovingly to those struggling with questions about faith are gifts to the church . . . *Sorting through Worldviews* . . . offers the possibility that followers of Jesus need not fear challenges to our faith but instead can engage with others with the confidence that God is at work even before our conversations begin."

—**MICHAEL MCNICHOLS**
Affiliate Assistant Professor, Fuller Theological Seminary

"There are many large books on apologetics covering every possible subject, and short ones that provide minimal help. Kline's approach is in-between . . . . His responsive approach is to ask penetrating questions to reach the central point of the issue. *Sorting through Worldviews* is clearly written; the arguments are easy to follow and helpful for anyone who wants to learn about and share their faith in Christ."

—**KENT MEADS**
Former Professor of Greek and Theology, San Jose Bible College

"I recommend *Sorting through Worldviews* to anyone investigating or defending Christianity. Kline has used his many years of investigative experience to present a well-developed yet straightforward method to look at serious questions that demand thoughtful answers. The chapters are concise and focus on what is vital in defending the faith. I trust all who read this book will use the teaching for personal and corporate betterment."

—**SCOTT LEMENAGER**
Special Assistant to the President,
Evangelical Church Alliance International

"Rick Kline is a gifted Christian thinker who refuses to shy away from difficult conversations. *Sorting through Worldviews* combines the church's wisdom with life anecdotes to equip anyone looking to build confidence when it comes to engaging others in matters of faith. In an era of rapid spiritual shifts, many Christians mourn what's been lost in the world. Rick chooses to engage it. After reading his book, you will too!"

—**MARK WHITSEL**
Lead Pastor, Pleasant Hills Community Presbyterian Church

Sorting through Worldviews

How to Give Reasonable Responses
in Defense of Christianity

Rick Kline

WIPF & STOCK · Eugene, Oregon

SORTING THROUGH WORLDVIEWS
How to Give Reasonable Responses in Defense of Christianity

Copyright © 2022 Rick Kline. All rights reserved. Except for brief quotations in critical publications or reviews, no part of this book may be reproduced in any manner without prior written permission from the publisher. Write: Permissions, Wipf and Stock Publishers, 199 W. 8th Ave., Suite 3, Eugene, OR 97401.

Wipf & Stock
An Imprint of Wipf and Stock Publishers
199 W. 8th Ave., Suite 3
Eugene, OR 97401

www.wipfandstock.com

PAPERBACK ISBN: 978-1-6667-3665-6
HARDCOVER ISBN: 978-1-6667-9534-9
EBOOK ISBN: 978-1-6667-9535-6

03/04/22

All Bible quotations, unless otherwise designated, are from the New International Version®, NIV®. Copyright © 1973, 1978, 1984, 2011 by Biblica, Inc.® Used by permission of Zondervan. All rights reserved worldwide.

Bible quotations designated as ESV are from the Holy Bible, English Standard Version®, copyright © 2001 by Crossway Bibles, a publishing ministry of Good News Publishers. Used by permission. All rights reserved.

Bible quotations designated as NET are from the New English Translation Bible®. Copyright © 2005 by Biblical Studies Press, LLC. www.bible.org. All rights reserved.

Bible quotations designated as KJV are from The Holy Bible, King James Version. Nashville: Nelson, 2016.

Bible quotations designated as NWT are from the New World Translation of the Holy Scriptures. Copyright @ 1961 by Watch Tower Bible and Tract Society of New York. Used by permission. All rights reserved.

To my wife, Sheryl, for her love, kindness, and patient coaching:
"You surpass them all"
(Prov 31:29)

Contents

Acknowledgments | ix
Abbreviations | xi

1   The Role of Questions and Answers | 1
    My Story behind the Method of Asking Questions

2   Truth Requires Investigation | 4
    Discerning Contradictions, Paradoxes, and Personal Feelings

3   Truth and the Scientific Method | 9
    Discerning if the Empirical Method Provides Ultimate Truth

4   Sorting through the Options | 14
    How to Find Truth by the Process of Elimination

5   The Option of Pantheism | 18
    Either the Universe Itself Is God or It Is Not:
    Analyzing Option 1(a) from Chapter 4

6   The Option of an Infinite Regress | 22
    Either the Universe Began or It Has Been in Existence Eternally:
    Analyzing Option 1(b) from Chapter 4

7   The Option of a Self-Created Universe | 28
    Either the Universe Created Itself or It Had a Creator:
    Analyzing Option 2(a) from Chapter 4

8   The Option of a Divinely Created Universe | 36
    Either the Universe Had a Creator/God or It Did Not:
    Analyzing Option 2(b) from Chapter 4

9   The Trinity and the Deity of Christ | 44
    Living with Paradoxes in the Personal Nature of God

10 Jehovah's Witnesses | 54
    Their View of Christ and Maintaining a Meaningful Dialogue

11 Mormons | 66
    Their Religious System and Staying on Track in a Dialogue

12 Islam | 79
    Basic Beliefs, the Quran, and Calmly Conversing with Muslims

13 Conversing with the Jewish Traditions | 88
    The Three Jewish Worldviews and Jesus as Messiah

14 The Eastern Religious Worldview | 95
    Karma, Luck, and New Age Mystical Spirituality

15 The "All Ways Lead to God" Idea and Zen Buddhism | 108
    Dissecting the Self-Contradiction of Religious Pluralism

16 God's Goodness vs. Evil and Suffering | 114
    If God Is Good, Then How Can There Be Evil and Suffering?

17 Salvation Is Not by Personal Merit | 126
    Discerning Whether Humans Must Earn Merit with God

18 Absolutes vs. Relativism | 130
    The Case for Universal, Objective, and Absolute Truth

19 Genesis, the Big Bang, and Moral Origins | 141
    The Contradictions of a God-less View of Human Origins

20 The Reliability of the Bible Showing Jesus as Lord | 151
    The Bible's Relevance as the Source of Spiritual Truth

21 Liar, Lunatic, Legend, or Lord | 158
    Options Regarding the Nature of Jesus

Glossary | 163
Bibliography | 165

Acknowledgments

I AM FOREVER INDEBTED to the loving persistence of my cousin, Leni Carter, who answered my stubborn objections to Christianity, and led me to accept Christ over fifty years ago.

To those who read, critiqued, and wrote endorsements to this book: thank you for sharing your time, wisdom, and knowledge.

To the Wipf and Stock editing team for their kind and timely help to produce this book.

Special thanks to Ray Beeson for years of encouragement to "write a book" and then the thousands of hours with me, wrestling with how to succinctly express theological concepts.

Much gratitude is expressed to my friend, Mike Huard, for his life-changing conversation with me outside of a small church in 1974 (briefly narrated in chapter 1).

Abbreviations

NT   New Testament of the Bible
OT   Old Testament of the Bible (the Hebrew Scriptures)

Abbreviations of OT Books

Genesis	Gen	1 Chronicles	1 Chr
Exodus	Exod	2 Chronicles	2 Chr
Leviticus	Lev	Ezra	Ezra
Numbers	Num	Nehemiah	Neh
Deuteronomy	Deut	Esther	Esth
Joshua	Josh	Job	Job
Judges	Judg	Psalm	Ps (Pss when multiple chapters are cited)
Ruth	Ruth		
1 Samuel	1 Sam	Proverbs	Prov
2 Samuel	2 Sam	Ecclesiastes	Eccl
1 Kings	1 Kgs	Song of Solomon	Song
2 Kings	2 Kgs	Isaiah	Isa

Abbreviations

Jeremiah	Jer	Jonah	Jonah
Lamentations	Lam	Micah	Mic
Ezekiel	Ezek	Nahum	Nah
Daniel	Dan	Habakkuk	Hab
Hosea	Hos	Zephaniah	Zeph
Joel	Joel	Haggai	Hag
Amos	Amos	Zechariah	Zech
Obadiah	Obad	Malachi	Mal

Abbreviations of NT Books

Matthew	Matt	1 Timothy	1 Tim
Mark	Mark	2 Timothy	2 Tim
Luke	Luke	Titus	Titus
John	John	Philemon	Phlm
Acts	Acts	Hebrews	Heb
Romans	Rom	James	Jas
1 Corinthians	1 Cor	1 Peter	1 Pet
2 Corinthians	2 Cor	2 Peter	2 Pet
Galatians	Gal	1 John	1 John
Ephesians	Eph	2 John	2 John
Philippians	Phil	3 John	3 John
Colossians	Col	Jude	Jude
1 Thessalonians	1 Thess	Revelation	Rev
2 Thessalonians	2 Thess		

1

The Role of Questions and Answers
My Story behind the Method of Asking Questions

Loss of Hope Countered by Truth

IN THE SPRING OF 1974, I was a twenty-three-year-old sailor stationed on a navy base in California and living in a base dorm room. I was planning to be discharged in August and then move to Pennsylvania to attend a Bible college. But I knew nothing about making this transition. I had no place to live, no job waiting, and little money. This produced a sense of uncertainty and fear that degenerated into despondency. These conflicts overwhelmed my feelings of spiritual passion.

During the previous three years, I had been enthusiastically involved in Christian service and teaching Bible studies. I read books by Christian authors on defending Christianity against objections to it (a discipline known as *apologetics*). The authors taught me to ask people *questions* when an objection to Christianity was proposed and, based on their *answers*, to ask more questions and then to provide a reasonable response. This process of *questions and answers* became my way of guiding someone to think about their non-Christian worldview (how one interprets life; a philosophy of life), and to consider Christianity as truth regarding spiritual matters. In spite of having read these faith-affirming books, I sensed fear and despondency over my uncertain future. I lost hope that God would solve this

Sorting through Worldviews

dilemma before August. I believed Christianity to be true but had no corresponding feelings. This was an entirely new predicament for me.

While sitting one evening in my dorm room feeling hopeless, a thought came to me: "Now I know why people commit suicide." This thought was not from an arousal to suicide. Instead, it was awareness that the loss of hope can drive someone to suicide. I had adopted a perspective of pessimism—a termination of the imagination.

I concealed my depression and absence of spiritual enthusiasm by continuing in Christian service until one night in June. I was talking with an older friend while we stood outside of a church in Camarillo, California, waiting for the church service to begin. I expressed my conflicts and told him that it made no sense to me that Christianity could be true without having the feelings to go along with it.

He asked me if something could be true without stirring any emotion, like, it's true that the earth is round, but not feel enthusiasm about it.

"Of course," I said.

"So Christianity can be true whether you feel it or not, right?" he asked.

I agreed.

He asked me, "Do you doubt that Christianity is true?"

I told him that I had considered opposing worldviews, although none cancelled my faith. But I had no spiritual passion and felt fearful. "What do you fear?" he asked.

I said that I feared "not knowing what's next."

He asked, "Would your circumstances be different if you felt different?"

"Probably not," I replied.

While he asked more questions, and I gave answers, I had the thought: "I feel like I'm talking to myself." He was using my own technique of asking questions to lead me to see things differently. No one had ever done this with me before. As we talked, he helped me see that pessimism is mistaking today as a permanent state of affairs.

No matter how depressed I felt, I did not come upon any argument against Christianity that destroyed my faith. The principles of apologetics enabled me to see the biblical narratives as true regardless of my lack of enthusiastic feelings. My faith was reasonable, even though I was still uncertain about my future.

In July, my own pastor told me to contact a friend of his who pastored another local church and who was looking for someone to fill a youth pastor position. My pastor said that he had recommended me to his friend. I met with this other pastor who offered me the position with a salary. I accepted the offer, and upon completion of my naval enlistment, I began my new role in a new church. God solved my dilemma about what to do with my future in a way I never expected.

I stayed in California, was ordained as a minister, continued in various ministries, worked in the title insurance industry, and then became a police officer for twenty years, retiring as a detective. During all this, I went to college and completed seminary courses. My wife and I now live in the Pittsburgh, Pennsylvania, area.

Questions and Answers Help Sort Out the Truth

My friend confirmed to me that the process of asking questions is a valuable way to engage someone in a peaceful conversation in order to guide them to *rethink* their perspective before I begin dispensing information to them. This method worked for me and was pivotal for a renewal of hope. The question-and-answer method is a nonconfrontational way to talk with someone holding a counter-Christian worldview. We can give an argument for the Christian faith without being argumentative.

Author Gregory Koukl says that to argue is to state a viewpoint, and "arguments are good things . . . because [argument] helps us determine what is true and discard what is false."[1] To argue in favor of Christianity is to calmly present a view.

This book contains conversations I have had with people who hold various non-Christian worldviews. I listened to their views during these conversations, then asked questions to draw out the underlying worldview position they held, and finally proposed the Christian alternative. This is a calm way to share our faith based on three simple concepts about Christianity. First, it is reasonable. Second, it is free of mutually exclusive concepts (contradictions). And third, it is consistent with how humans live.

Christian reasoning serves faith; it is not a substitute for faith. The Spirit does the converting while using us as tools. These conversations do not need to be emotional episodes, as we shall see in the following chapters.

Enjoy the journey.

---

1. Koukl, *Tactics*, 23, 33. Koukl is the founder of Stand to Reason (www.str.org), a website dedicated to helping Christians think clearly on various social and spiritual issues.

2

Truth Requires Investigation

Discerning Contradictions, Paradoxes, and Personal Feelings

A Good Question Leads to Self-Examination

I TOLD MY WIFE that I enjoyed spending a lot of time with the grandchildren when they visit. She asked, "Really? Then why do you go into your study shortly after they arrive?" She nailed me. A simple question made me reexamine myself and rethink my statement. I realized that my practice and my statement were inconsistent; my statement was false.

We must realize that *what is contradictory must be false*. This principle applies to examining our personal life and examining a *worldview* (a philosophy of life). We can apply two overarching questions to determine if a worldview is valid. First, is the view free of contradiction so that the view can be lived out consistently? Secondly, is the view reasonably verifiable, or is it just mystical superstition?

Worldview Discovery Takes Exploration

A man standing outside of a forest can say, "This forest is beautiful," but this is only a simplistic viewpoint, since he did not enter the forest. Looking into worldviews is similar to venturing into the forest. To examine if a worldview is universally true, we must venture into it to see if the viewpoint can be consistently maintained.

I had a discussion with a woman about whether Christianity gives us ultimate truth about life. She said that there was no ultimate truth. This was her simplistic worldview, which I explored by a few questions.

"Are you saying that seeking ultimate truth is meaningless because ultimate truth does not exist in the universe?" I asked.

"That's right," she said.

"But doesn't your view have an ultimate meaning *for you*? If so, how would you know it has meaning in a universe where ultimate truth is meaningless?"

"You're just trying to trick me," she said.

Actually, I was trying to show her that her theory that a meaningless universe had meaning for her was contradictory and that she would not be able to know the theory was true in a meaningless universe. That is, the theory that we live in a meaningless universe is a theory that is meaningless.

She lived as if there were ultimate meaning for her life while simultaneously denying there was ultimate meaning. This is an example of contradictory thinking that affected her worldview.

The physical sciences tell us truth about most aspects of the physical realm by testing a theory over and over. We know that the law of gravity exists on earth, because rocks drop every time we release them. If I hypothesize that rocks can fly by their own initiative, but experiments contradict this, then the concept is inconsistent with life's experiences. I should abandon this hypothesis, because it is untrue.

Considering a realm beyond the physical is called *metaphysical* study (*meta*, beyond), and uses the nonphysical method for determining a truth claim: logical reasoning. If we follow out a worldview argument—a mental experiment—and eventually see that the concept is inconsistent with how we live, or outright contradicts reality, then the concept shows a strong gravitational pull to falsehood. We should abandon the worldview.

The Claim That Science Dispels Religion as Superstitious

A close friend told me over lunch in a restaurant that he is an atheist, because "science makes things simple and refutes superstition." He said, for example, people once thought bad weather came from angry gods, but science shows weather is from natural weather patterns. Science exposes religious beliefs as "complicated superstitions." That was his worldview theory. I did not have an immediate response, since I had not heard this idea before. I sat back for a minute, sipped some coffee, and stalled to think; then I picked up a napkin.

I said, "The napkin appears to be a simple paper product." I suggested that scientists can scientifically explain to us that napkins are composed of molecules made of atoms with even smaller subatomic particles. The closer a scientist looks at a napkin, the more complicated, not the simpler, it becomes. My friend's theory that religious faith is complicated but that science makes things *simple* is not universally true. Science does the opposite of his theory. Who thinks quantum physics, for example, is simple? Physicist Christophe Galfard quotes Einstein as saying to students after a lecture in quantum physics: "If you have understood me, then I haven't been clear."[1] Science does dispel superstition, but science also reveals that more mysteries exist that do not contradict the religious faith realm.

The Contradiction and the Self-Refuting Statement

A contradiction is a statement that is impossible to be true. A contradiction means that if one statement is true, then its opposite is false. The statement "Bob is a married bachelor," for example, asserts two mutually exclusive concepts, because being married excludes its opposite: a bachelor. Truth is exclusive. Not every worldview can be true.

A basic rule of reason is the *rule of noncontradiction*. This means that any argument that is contradictory must be false. For example, a square circle cannot exist, because the nature of a square consists of four corners, and the nature of a circle is that it has no corners. Also, for example, the earth cannot be a cube with eight corners and simultaneously be a sphere without corners. Both examples violate the rule of noncontradiction. Ignoring this rule is to think that reason is not real. Philosophy professor Siu-Fan Lee defines a contradiction as "a statement that is always false."[2]

A *self-refuting* statement is another way to see a false concept. Consider the statement "Everything is an illusion." This statement is self-refuting, because thinking is involved in the statement. If all thought is an illusion, then the statement itself is an illusion. The statement destroys itself like

---

1. Galfard, *Universe in Your Hand*, 168.
2. Lee, *Logic*, 308.

Superman building his fortress using kryptonite. Chapter 18 contains more examples of self-refuting statements.

For Christians to gently point out that a statement is nonsense is not being rude. It even finds support from the atheist Bertrand Russell who wrote, "Nonsense of a sort has always been recognized: consider 'I married a prime number' and 'Virtue is triangular.'"[3]

The Paradox

Paradoxes are views that seem as opposites, but a paradox does not contain two mutually exclusive concepts as a contradiction does. Judgment and mercy seem like opposites. However, both can work simultaneously, such as a judge sentencing a felon to ten years in prison instead of fifteen, due to a sense of mercy. Paradoxes are like conflicted brain teasing, because they contain "the idea of conflict."[4]

Personal Feelings Do Not Make a Statement True

When a child concludes that two apples plus two apples equals seven apples, the child is wrong. Seven does not exist as an answer, even if the child feels love for the number seven because seven is the jersey number of his/her favorite professional athlete. Since four is the true sum, then it is false that the answer is any other sum. Contradictions cannot be overcome by personal feelings. A contradictory worldview is false regardless of how a person feels about their worldview. Ignoring the rule of noncontradiction produces the view that nonsense can make sense. A person may say that they feel a particular idea is true but have no thoughts or reasons for the contradictory truth claim. To *feel* something is not always to *think* something. God gave us a mind as a tool to know truth.

Investigating a Common Statement of Skepticism

Suppose someone says to you, "We should be skeptical of everything." Two problems leap out with this statement. First, to be consistent, skeptics should also believe that you should be skeptical of their skepticism, so why

3. Smart, "Province of Philosophy," 15.
4. Cargile, "Paradoxes," 642.

would skeptics think you should agree with them? Philosopher Peter Kreeft says, "The skeptic is not skeptical enough, for he is not really skeptical of his skepticism."[5] Secondly, it is a claim that truth is private and relative; so why would skeptics think their skepticism applies to you, too?

Skepticism leads to disunity of thought, because what is considered to be true is arbitrarily picked out from all things skeptical.[6] Even if we do not know the truth of all things with certainty, we do not want to conclude that we are certain that all things are uncertain.[7]

The coming chapters will show how Christianity is consistently practical and will answer questions and concerns about life.

---

5. Kreeft, *Summa Philosophica*, 129.
6. Copan, *True for You*, 26–39.
7. Brown, *Miracles and Critical Mind*, 27.

3

Truth and the Scientific Method
Discerning if the Empirical Method Provides Ultimate Truth

Science as Ultimate Truth Is Not a Scientific Statement

IN CHAPTER 2, WE saw that asking questions to investigate a claim is not difficult, yet it is necessary to see if a claim leads to a contradiction. If so, then the worldview claim is false. This can be illustrated by the following conversation I had over lunch with a friend who claimed to be a God-skeptic.[1] He proposed that the scientific method of *empiricism* (truth is determined by verifiable evidence) was his method to decide what was ultimately true, and this method also applied to the nonphysical realm.

Empiricism is "any view which bases our knowledge . . . on experience through the traditional five senses."[2] Colin Brown states that empiricism came from a quest to find true knowledge, so "the empiricists stressed . . . experience."[3] Empiricism is said to be "the theory that experience rather than reason is the source of knowledge."[4]

---

1. Not all atheists absolutely deny God's existence; they are just skeptical of it.
2. Lacey, "Empiricism," 242.
3. Brown, *Philosophy and Christian Faith*, 60.
4. Hamlyn, "Empiricism," 499.

To clarify what I understood my friend to say, I asked, "Do you think that your statement, 'The scientific empirical method tells us ultimate truth' is, in fact, a *true* statement?"

"Yes," he said.

"All right then. So, what empirical method did you use to know that your statement is a true statement?" I asked.

He looked at me and finally said, "None."

I said that he could not say that his statement was really a true statement since he did not verify its truth by the empirical method. He could not apply his own standard of verification to his own concept, so his proposition was unverifiable.

I pointed out that Christians are not anti-empirical. We use a spoon, for example, not a fork, to eat soup, and dig holes with a shovel, not a toothpick. Empiricism is valuable but limited as an ultimate truth-bearer. Over the years, we continued to talk on these topics, but as of this writing, he remains a God-skeptic.

Beauty and Love as Mystical, Not Empirical

I asked this same friend another question as a means of exploring his proposition that empiricism is the only source for truth. I asked, "Does beauty exist?"

He said that it did.

I asked, "How did science verify that beauty exists?"

"We are all a collection of molecules; the sense of beauty is in the physical realm," he responded.

"Does this also apply to love?"

He said that both were just a "chemical reaction" to some stimuli within us.

I asked what his wife would think if she said to him, "I love you," and he responded with something to this effect: "I sense a strong chemical and molecular reaction within me provoking a favorable sensation towards you."

He laughed and conceded that this response would not work.

Not all things we believe to be true are empirically verifiable. There is no such thing as the weight of beauty, or the color of love, or the fragrance of a rectangle. A worldview claiming that life's experiences are reduced to natural chemical reactions should prompt suspicion when we cannot live consistently with such a worldview.

Truth and the Scientific Method

God Is Not an Exhibitionist

"Can you prove to me that God exists, to eliminate my skepticism?" a man asked me as I handed him some Christian literature. I answered the question with a question. "Can you tell me what you consider proof, and I'll see if I can give it to you?" There was no response. Some people ask for proof without knowing what they are asking for. To help the conversation continue, I held out one of my hands with the palm up and asked him a question. "Suppose a glass containing a hot fudge sundae popped into existence in my palm in answer to prayer. Would that be proof?" He said, "Maybe." I said that he would not get his proof, because God is not an amusing exhibitionist.

Truth Is Not Always Verified by Scientific Experiments

While having a meal with one of my nonreligious college philosophy professors, I claimed that the universe seemed to have a Creator: God. He retorted, "You cannot use metaphysical arguments in philosophy; stick to what is known empirically!" He was saying that I cannot appeal to the nonphysical realm regarding the issues of life, that I should stick to the physical realm instead. This is a strange argument for a philosophy professor, since the word philosophy means the *love of wisdom,* and this is in the metaphysical realm. The love of philosophy is not subject to empirical analysis.[5] I did not succeed in changing his viewpoint.

Scientific experiments—the empirical method—for knowledge are vital for the realm of the physical world. They do not, however, answer for ultimate truth outside of the physical realm.

Saturn

Never pass up the opportunity to answer a question with a question, because you never know where it will lead, as shown by the following story. A few years ago, when I was a detective, I was sitting at my desk in a large room the detectives called the "bull pen." Another detective came over to me and commented on the picture of the planet Saturn pinned to my cubicle wall.

---

5. Philosophy is from two Greek words: *philos,* love of, and *sophia,* wisdom (Reese, *Dictionary of Philosophy and Religion,* 573).

"Why Saturn?" he asked.

I leaned back in my chair and asked, "Well, it's real and awesome, and evidence of God's creativity with the rings and all, don't you think?"

"It is cool, but we don't know if it's evidence of God, since God's existence cannot be verified," he said.

"How empirical of you," I responded.

"Huh?"

"Empiricism," I said. "It seems that you're saying that only what can be verified to be true, is actually true."

"I guess that's what I'm saying," he said.

"Okay, but if what is true is only known via verification, then how do you know that your statement itself is true without it also being verified? But we cannot go on and on trying to verify each statement, or we'll never know anything for sure."

"What?" he asked.

"Look at it like this. Saturn's existence is verified as a physical object. God, however, is not a physical object, but does that mean we have no basis to believe he exists? It seems like what we can actually see is itself evidence of God's existence."

As a Catholic, he believed in God. The discussion continued, and he said that this gave him a desire to read more of the Bible for truth lying outside of the physical world.

What about Evidence?

Some scientists want verifiable evidence of God's existence before they believe that God exists.[6] Consider this argument: "I don't believe in God, because there is no evidence of God." The underlying claim is that belief in something must be based on *evidence*. Note that evidence is the criterion for what is believed. But no evidence exists to disprove God. If evidence is needed for a belief, then what evidence is there *not* to believe in God? There is none. For the skeptic to say that he or she believes only on the basis of evidence, and then say he or she believes God does not exist without evidence—this is contradictory. There must be some other reason for the skeptic to believe that God does not exist, since atheism is not based on evidence. This other reason is that the person has chosen not to believe God exists as a philosophical worldview. Jeffrey Russell says, "There is no

6. Stenger, *God: The Failed Hypothesis*, 22.

Truth and the Scientific Method

empirical proof of atheism," and to assert that God does not exist is "not a scientific statement but an ideological one."[7]

Christians appreciate evidence, just as Jesus did. In John 14:11, Jesus said to believe in what he said, "or at least believe on the *evidence* of the miracles." And Jesus "gave many convincing *proofs*" of his resurrection by appearing to people (Acts 1:3; emphasis added). Psalm 19 states that the existence of the heavens declares that God exists. Proof of God's existence, however, is not generally relegated to concrete proof, like proving a specific rock is made of granite. God is not an object, so evidence comes in other forms, as we will see.

We have briefly considered whether the empirical option for ultimate truth can be consistently maintained; but it cannot. The next chapter will outline the four basic *options* to account for the existence of the universe, and then we will follow each view out to see if the particular view is contradictory or not.

7. Russell, *Exposing Myths about Christianity*, 139.

4

Sorting through the Options

How to Find Truth by the Process of Elimination

The Value of Considering Options

Dismissing an opposing view to our Christian faith should be taken seriously. In the previous two chapters, we considered whether the scientific view for determining ultimate truth—truth beyond the physical realm—gave all the answers for life. It did not. Now we will consider the four overarching views for the existence of the universe. Listing options is a truth-seeking method.

Peacefully Eliminating Options to Settle on Truth

Before I became a detective, I drove a marked police car, as all patrol officers do, and I was dispatched to investigate two subjects in a parked vehicle, possibly smoking narcotics. As I stopped my car behind their car, I saw a man in the driver's seat and a woman seated next to him. Both of them were making movements as if putting something under the front seat. Then the woman exited the car and walked into a house. The man stayed in the driver's seat. Two other officers arrived to assist. I approached the car and asked the man to step out and come to the sidewalk, which he did. A check on the car's license plate showed this man as the car's owner. My partners saw two small bags, containing a white substance, and a pipe in the front seat, in plain view.

"So . . . what's the story with you and the woman in the car with drugs?" I asked.

He proposed the following story: they were just talking; he didn't know the woman's name; he drove her to the location, so the woman could meet someone; and if there were drugs in the car, they belonged to someone else.

I calmly said, "Your story makes no sense based on the observations of me and my partners." I suggested that there were *four options* as to why his story made no sense and asked if he would like to hear them. He said that he would, so I began my list of options.

"Option one: *I'm* too stupid to understand you. Is that true?"

"No."

"All right then. Option two: *You're* delusional, but you do not appear to be this kind of person. You seem like an intelligent guy."

He agreed.

"Okay. Option three as to why your story makes no sense is because we're in an alternate universe where nothing makes sense. Do you think so?"

"I don't think so," he said.

"Well then, this leads us to the fourth and final option. The only reason your story makes no sense is because it's a false story." I asked him if there was another option, but he could not think of one, so I asked for the true story. He admitted that he was not telling me the truth and told me the name of his female friend and that they were smoking his narcotics.

We can use *commonsense* principles of reason without the danger of becoming angry, emotional, or insulting. Sometimes a proposition makes no sense because the proposition is contradictory and, therefore, false.

How can we apply this principle of logically *sorting through options* in order to determine if it is more likely that God exists than that God does not exist? In regards to the universe, how many options do we have to explain its existence?

The Chart of Options

During a conversation in a coffee shop about God's existence, my friend said, "I want proof." I said that concrete proof was unrealistic, so I suggested a simpler method. We could list *options* to explain the existence of the universe, analyze them, and eliminate the contradictory and, therefore, false ideas. This method would lead us to one concept that is more *reasonable* and more *likely* to be true. He consented to this method, so I placed a napkin down and drew this simple *Chart of Options*.[1]

The Universe...			
1. Did not begin		2. Began	
(a)	(b)	(a)	(b)
Pantheism	Infinite regression	Created itself	Was created

I turned the napkin around and showed my friend what I wrote and said, "These are the only worldviews available to explain how we arrived here at this table *today*."

I advanced the idea that there are two overarching options: Option 1 or Option 2. Each has two sub-options, making *four total options* shown as 1(a), 1(b), 2(a), 2(b).

I asked if I had missed any options. He said that I had listed all of them.

Two Overarching Options for the Origin of the Universe

Option 1: The universe *did not begin* because it is eternal.
Or:
Option 2: The universe *began* in space and time.
Under Option 1, there are only two sub-options for an *eternally* existing universe:
(a) The universe is God (*pantheism*);[2] "God ... is the same as nature."[3]
Or:
(b) Today came from a beginning-less series of causes and effects, an *infinite regression* of causes and effects.
Under Option 2, there are only two sub-options for a *beginning* of the universe:
(a) The universe popped into existence; it *created itself.*
Or:
(b) The universe *was created* by a Creator.

   1. My concept of this chart of is from Turek and Geisler, *I Don't Have Enough Faith*, 93.
   2. Pantheism is from two Greek words: *pan*, everything, and *theos*, god. Pantheism means that the universe itself is god or that the universe and god are without distinction (Reese, *Dictionary of Philosophy and Religion*, 546).
   3. Kessler, *Voices of Wisdom*, 632.

Sorting through the Options

To Restate and Summarize the Four Options

Option 1(a): The universe did not begin in space and time, because the universe itself is God.

Option 1(b): The universe did not begin in space and time, because the universe has eternally existed, without a God of any kind as a cause of it.

Option 2(a): The universe began in space and time, because the universe created itself; it popped into existence on its own; there was and is now no Creator God of any kind as a cause.

Option 2(b): The universe began in space and time, because the universe was created by a Creator God as a cause of it.

What Is Meant by a Beginning?

When we speak of any *thing* such as physical matter, a force, gravity, as having a *beginning*, we mean that this thing has an origin in space and time. According to *Merriam-Webster's Collegiate Dictionary*, to *begin* means "to come into existence . . . to have a starting point." In other words, for x (an atom, for example) to begin to exist in space and time, there was a prior state in which x did not exist in any form; otherwise, the word beginning has no meaning.

The Truth of a Worldview Is in Its Consistency with Life

To test the coherence of a particular worldview, the worldview must be contrasted with other views. A worldview is coherent if it is consistent with how we live. I briefly went through these four options with my friend.

The following four chapters examine these options in more detail to see which one is more likely, or more probable, to be true. Included are summaries of dialogues I have had with people holding these worldviews, using the method of asking questions. I intend to show that Option 2(b) is the most reasonable option, because it is free of inherent contradictions and is consistent with how we live.

5

The Option of Pantheism

Either the Universe Itself Is God or It Is Not: Analyzing Option 1(a) from Chapter 4

Pantheism

I WILL BEGIN WITH option 1(a) shown in the Chart of Options in chapter 4, because it is the easiest to see how inconsistent it is in contrast to how people live. Additional comments on pantheism are in chapter 14 regarding the Eastern religious worldview.

Pantheism is "the doctrine that . . . nature . . . is identical with God."[1] This means that nature, like electrons, rocks, animals, humans, *is* Divine, because "all is God, and God is all."[2] Since pantheism makes no distinction between God and the universe, the miracle of Genesis 1:1 that states "God created" the cosmos would be impossible, because there is no God *outside* of the cosmos to create it.[3] The Bible and pantheism are contradictory ideas.

Some form of pantheism is found in Hinduism, Buddhism, and New Age mysticism, among other worldviews.

---

1. Mautner, *Dictionary of Philosophy*, 448.
2. Geisler, *Baker Encyclopedia of Christian Apologetics*, 580.
3. Geisler, *Baker Encyclopedia of Christian Apologetics*, 580.

The Option of Pantheism

What's Wrong with God That He Doesn't Know Who He Is?

During a college philosophy class on Eastern religions that I attended, the professor explained Hindu pantheism using fire and sparks as an analogy. The essence of a spark from a camp fire is the same as the fire itself. Our self (a spark) *is* god (the fire), without distinction. The spirit of divinity is in everything and everyone.

I asked the following question: "The majority of people do not believe they are divine. If everyone is divine, but we don't know it, what's wrong with God that he doesn't know who he is?" The professor asked if anyone in the class had an answer. No one did, so the professor went on with his lecture, ignoring the implication that God has an ignorance factor.

Pantheism Implies Universal Equalization

In defense of pantheism, a Buddhist friend told me that the universe is set up so that when we eat vegetables for nourishment and we eventually die, we return to the earth to nourish other vegetables, and the cycle goes on. "Everything is equalized," he said.

I asked: "What about fighting?"

"What do you mean?" he asked.

I proposed that since he and I are equally divine, then hitting him seemed as if God was hitting himself, and if so, how can we object to physical violence? If all things are equalized, doesn't this imply that all actions are God's actions, and if so, how can we distinguish between actions as either good or bad? My friend admitted that he had no objective standard to distinguish good from evil, but some acts do seem evil. I pointed out that we all live as if there were a real qualitative moral distinction between actions. I alleged that pantheism is contradictory, because it asserts a concept that all actions are equal, but humans live as though evil and good are really different. Pantheism is inconsistent within its own philosophy.

Pantheism Reduces Everything in the Cosmos to the Same Level

Consider the following implications if pantheism is true.

Everything that happens is determined to happen. If God *is* the universe, then there is no such thing as chance, accidents, or contingent events. All events are predetermined to happen, since all events *are* God. Pantheism is determinism.

The universe is reduced to the same level of value and worth. Rocks and humans would share the same intrinsic value, because there could not be more of God in a human than in a rock. If the rock is divine, then being hit with a rock by an immoral human would be no different than being hit by a nonmoral, or morally neutral, meteorite. Do pantheists think that someone hitting them with a rock is morally neutral? We all live in the world as if there is a moral distinction between how rocks hit us, which distinction would not exist if pantheism is true.

All human thoughts are God's thoughts. If everything is God, then our thoughts and God's thoughts would be synonymous. But pantheists believe that some ideologies, like racism, are wrong and that some answers in a math test are wrong. Pantheists do not live as if there are no wrong answers.

All belief systems are reduced to the same level of truth. If pantheism is true, then all religious views would be correct, since all thinking would be God's thinking and equally valid. However, pantheists do not live as if this is true. Hindus and Buddhists, for example, disagree on concepts of God. Wouldn't contradictory religious views be God disagreeing with himself? Pantheists assert that all is God but then disagree with me if I say they are wrong. How can they defend their view against my view if my view is equally true? Pantheists oppose what they think is a wrong belief, showing that they cannot live consistently with the view that everything is equally true.

All moral acts are reduced to mere events, leaving no distinction between good and evil. In a pantheistic universe, all acts would be God's acts. This makes mercy and cruelty equal. It follows that if God is all good and all acts are God's acts, then all actions are good. This eliminates the distinction between good and evil. Two implications result from this. First, *God would be impersonal.* Pantheism reduces good and evil to a *co-equal* level; therefore, there would be no preference for either one over the other. A power without preference is impersonal. It is illogical to contend that an impersonal force prefers one act over another act, when all acts are co-equal. Pantheism leaves us with no hope of a relationship with a personal God. Second, *God would be dualistic.* In pantheism, good and evil are *co-eternal* moral attributes of God, because neither preceded the other. If so, then there is no hope that good eventually wins over evil, or that suffering will end. Pantheism leaves us with an endless future of futile struggle.

The Option of Pantheism

Why Are There Atheists?

Atheists are those who deny that God exists. If all humans *are* God, how can there be atheists who deny the existence of God? If atheists *are* divine—God—how could God deny his own existence? The existence of even one atheist shows that pantheism is a contradiction.

The "Lie Detector" Machine

I spoke with a detective who is an expert in conducting polygraph examinations. He told me that the device can detect physiological changes in a person when the person resorts to a lie and/or deception when answering a question. I asked the expert a hypothetical question: "In a pantheistic universe, doesn't it seem odd that our bodies react to a lie; wouldn't lying be natural?" He said that he had no theological opinion on this, but, of course, I do. If pantheism is true, then all that we think and say should be exactly what the universal all-pervading soul thinks and says, so why would the device detect lying? Lying and truth would be equal in a pantheistic universe. But pantheists believe lying is wrong, since lying is the opposite of telling the truth, and truth-telling is thought to be morally good. Pantheists do not live consistently in a world in which lying and telling the truth are naturally equal.

Humans Live in Contradiction to Pantheism

Pantheists do not live as if there is no distinction between good and evil, between mercy and cruelty, between giving and stealing, between telling the truth and lying. Pantheists, for example, exalt selfless acts of sacrifice but condemn tyranny, imprison murderers, fight against a pandemic disease. If all actions are God's actions, then wouldn't fighting evil and suffering be a fight against God?

The pantheistic worldview is outside of the way pantheists actually live. It is inconsistent with life's experience. Pantheism stands in contradiction to itself. A worldview that is contradictory must be false.

This eliminates option 1(a) from chapter 4 as an explanation for the existence of the universe.

Next we will consider option 1(b) to see if it makes sense that the *present day* could have come from a beginning-less process of cause and effects.

6

The Option of an Infinite Regress

Either the Universe Began or It Has Been in Existence Eternally: Analyzing Option 1(b) from Chapter 4

What the Term *Infinite Regression* Means

THOSE WHO DENY ALL religious explanations for the origin of the universe and deny the nonreligious view that the universe popped into existence on its own must then propose another worldview. The alternative worldview is this: the universe has always existed in a natural cause-and-effect series of events.

An infinite regression means that we cannot trace the events of the universe backwards to a first cause, because the universe has no first cause, no beginning, no starting point. It is a *beginning-less series of yesterdays*. For example, if you are reading this book on a Sunday, Sunday came because there was a yesterday—a Saturday; and before Saturday, there was a yesterday—a Friday; and so forth, going on infinitely in a reverse series of yesterdays. But it is impossible that an infinite amount of yesterdays leading up to today can be real, because in order to get to today, it was necessary to pass through a countable amount of yesterdays. But infinity is the opposite of anything that can be counted. Infinite yesterdays eliminates a first-day event, and without a first-day event, there is nothing to begin the chain

The Option of an Infinite Regress

of countable events that we call the passing of days. Our existence today contradicts an infinite amount of yesterdays.

The difficulty of discussing this is not because it is hard to understand—it is not—but because most people want to discuss infinity in the shortest amount of time.

Dominoes

A friend of mine and I were talking in the parking lot of a business. To refute my concept that the universe began with God, he proposed that the universe always existed. To clarify his position, I asked: "Do you mean that there has been an infinite series of past events leading to today—to now?"

He said, "Yes."

"If so, then we would not be talking *today*, because *now*, the present time, would not have arrived."

He looked at me as if I were the pope of the absurd and asked, "How do you figure that?"

"Well," I said, "imagine an infinite line of dominoes in front of us stretching from our left—the infinite past—and continuing on to our right—to the eternal future. Suppose these dominoes have been falling infinitely. How long would we have to stand here until we see the dominoes in front of us fall?"

He said, "A long time."

I unfurled the idea that we'd *never* see the dominoes fall, because the falling dominoes would never arrive at today, since their falling has been going on infinitely and infinity cannot be crossed. I continued by asking, "How long would we have to walk to our left in order to see falling dominoes?"

He didn't know.

I proposed that we would walk forever but never see falling dominoes, because no matter where we were on the infinite line of dominoes, there would be infinity before that. If we walked farther, there would be infinity before that, and on and on . . . infinitely. How would the dominoes even begin to fall, since there was no first cause that tipped the first domino?

I explained that if an infinite regression were true, we'd never arrive at today; but we are at today, standing in a parking lot; so the infinite regression theory is false. It is contradictory to think that today's universe moved forward from a beginning-less series of events.

He offered no rebuttal to my argument.

The domino illustration is from William Lane Craig who said, "The series of past events like . . . dominoes falling one after another until . . . today" is impossible, because "no series that is formed by adding one member after another can be actually infinite. For you cannot pass through an infinite number of elements one at a time."[1] In other words, infinity cannot be crossed.

Infinity Cannot Be Crossed, So Today Would Not Arrive

During a Bible study class, students and I were discussing how the current existence of the universe came to be what it is *today*. A student proposed the infinite regression theory. Instead of marching out biblical texts on creation in a warlike frontal assault, I asked her a few questions.

"How much time would it take to walk across this room, from wall to wall, which is about thirty feet of *actual* space?"

She said, "About five seconds."

"And I would need to complete the actual events of taking actual steps to cross the room?"

"Sure," she said.

"What if there were infinity to cross, how long would it take, and how many actual steps would I have to take to complete the journey—to traverse the room?"

"An infinite amount of steps," she said.

An "infinite amount" is correct, because wherever I might be, there is still infinity to go. No matter how long I had been walking, I would not have really gone anywhere. I would never arrive at any point.

We have to think of taking steps as actual events that takes time to do. But it is contradictory to think of infinity as something involving events in time, because infinity has no time. No actual events can take place in infinity, because there is no starting point from which progress is made to reach another point.

"Turn to page fifty in your Bible," I suggested. "If you were reading your Bible from page one, how did you arrive at page fifty?" I asked.

"From reading the previous forty-nine pages," she said.

That is exactly right. To read up to page fifty, it is necessary to pass through forty-nine *actual* previous pages. But if there were *infinite pages*,

1. Craig, *On Guard*, 83.

The Option of an Infinite Regress

you would never reach page fifty, because there are no actual number of pages to go through. No matter how many pages you flipped back to, there would still be infinite pages to flip back to. Since there is no first page, you could not advance through the book.[2]

In our world of actual space/time, we can complete a journey from point *a* to point *b*, because we can traverse this actual space, which also takes actual time. But infinity has no actual space and time. There is no starting point *a* and no eventual point *b* to reach. It is like a man hovering in space, attempting to jump, without a platform from which to launch. Or as philosophy professor J. P. Moreland observes, you could not reach the top of "an infinitely tall bottomless pit."[3] In order for the universe to exist today, it must have a jumping-off point. The student's proposition of an infinite series leading to today is contradictory, since it implies that infinity can be crossed without a jumping-off point. Infinity cannot be traversed.

Moreland and Craig explain the impossibility of traversing infinity. They write: "In order for us to have 'arrived' at today, temporal existence [must have] traversed an infinite number of prior events. But before the present event could arrive, the event immediately prior to it would have to arrive . . . and so on ad infinitum. No event could ever arrive, since before it could elapse, there will always be one more event that had to have happened first. Thus, if the series of past events were beginning-less, the present event could not have arrived, which is absurd."[4]

Craig points out the contradictory notion that an infinite past can end up at today by explaining that a "series of past events [coming] to an end in the present" is impossible, because "the infinite cannot come to an end."[5]

Today—an end—would never be reached in a universe with an infinite regression.

Examples Showing That Today Cannot Be from Infinite Events

Here are three examples to show that the reality of the present day contradicts the theory of an infinite regression of past events.

---

2. This example is from Geivett, "Kalaam Cosmological Argument," 65.
3. Moreland, "Arguments for Existence of God," 2.
4. Moreland and Craig, *Philosophical Foundations*, 473–74.
5. Craig, *Reasonable Faith*, 96.

Energy would have been used up an infinity ago. When a God-skeptic acquaintance proposed the infinite regression argument to me, I asked, "Is the sun using up its available energy, and will it eventually burn out?"

He said, "Yes, because science states that the sun will die in about five billion years from now."

"Is the sun part of the infinite regressive series of past events?"

He said that he thought so.

I said, "If so, the sun would have burned out in the infinite past. But the sun is still here." I suggested that the *present* sun stands in contradiction to an infinite regression of past events. Dean Overman puts it this way: "The universe could not be dissipating [using up itself] from infinity or it would have run down by now. Consequently, the universe had a beginning."[6]

An infinitely expanding universe is impossible. If the expanse has been going on infinitely, then the galaxies would be infinitely separated by now. But they are not. Overman states that because the universe has a "positive average expansion rate," an infinite past is impossible, since, if the universe is expanding, it is doing so from a beginning.[7] The universe cannot be infinitely old.

Current evolution in an infinite regression is impossible. If the present earth emerged from an infinite regression of past events, and life has been evolving in this series, everything would have evolved to perfection by now. But evolutionists state we are still evolving. How can we still be evolving, if we have been evolving in a beginning-less series of events? Since we have not completed evolution by now, according to evolutionists, then an infinite regress as an argument for the existence of the cosmos is contradictory.

What We Imagine Is Not Always Actual

What we imagine is sometimes impossible to be actual, or real. No *actual* finite events could have taken place from eternity. That is, the events cannot have actually happened in reality.

Can there be an *actual* infinite past? No, because an actual infinite past means that there is an actual countable amount of events from infinity. However, as Overman observes, no one can "count an actual infinite series of past events," because "to arrive at any particular point in time in a series of infinite events, one must already have counted an infinite number of

---

6. Overman, *Case for Existence of God*, 156.
7. Overman, *Case for Existence of God*, 37.

The Option of an Infinite Regress

events to get to that point."[8] It is contradictory to assert that actual countable events exist in an infinite series of events. A worldview that is contradictory must be false.

A Recurring Concept

This idea of an infinite regression is implied in the following chapters on Mormonism and Eastern religions. It is not an argument used only by atheists.

Conclusions So Far

Chapter 4 listed four options for the existence of the universe. Option 1(a) was eliminated in chapter 5. We have now eliminated option 1(b). Now we will turn to a discussion on whether the universe could have *created itself* from nothing.

---

8. Overman, *Case for Existence of God*, 49.

7

The Option of a Self-Created Universe

*Either the Universe Created Itself
or It Had a Creator:
Analyzing Option 2(a) from Chapter 4*

Intent of Chapters 7 and 8

IN CHAPTER 5, THE pantheistic view was discredited, because, among other things, it implies an *impersonal* god. In chapter 6, the infinite regression view was discredited, because it shows the impossibility that infinity can be traversed.

In chapters 7 and 8, we will examine if it is more reasonable to believe that the universe had a *God-less*—self-caused—beginning or if a *God-caused* beginning is more likely. First, we will examine the atheistic worldview that the universe *began* to exist without a God-cause.

The Meaning of a Self-Created Universe

A self-created, or a self-caused, universe is a *closed system*, which means that no spiritual Creator exists *outside* of the universe that created it from nothing. A "big bang" is given by some scientists for the beginning of the space/time universe.[1] This big bang is modestly described in an internet

1. Hawking, *Brief History of Time*; Hawking and Mlodinow, *Grand Design*.

article as the expansion of all the energy of the universe from a single infinitely dense point.[2]

Chance Plus Time

If the universe began with a God-less big bang event, then the beginning was accidental. It came into existence by pure chance. It began without a reasonable mind to cause it to begin in the first place; therefore, the universe has a nonrational beginning. This means that our present existence comes from *chance plus time*.

Some Christian scholars profess a big bang beginning by saying that God could have started with this event as his first creative act. For example, physicist Steven Ball writes that "it is clear that the Big Bang theory points to a moment of creation as described in Scripture, where the cause of it lies outside of the matter, space and time of our universe."[3]

I am not arguing for or against a God-caused big bang beginning. I am only challenging the idea that the big bang event was *not* God-caused.

Discussion on the Big Bang

In a short conversation, my friend "Joe" (not his real name) said that a Creator God was not necessary, because the big bang event was the beginning of space, time, matter, and forces like gravity. He said that the universe came from an infinitely dense singular point—a quantum fluctuation—producing the expansion of the universe. A quantum fluctuation is the idea that energy particles appear out of empty space. Joe's worldview is similar to that of Stephen Hawking who wrote that "the laws of nature in our universe arose from the big bang."[4]

"Are you saying, Joe, that the big bang event was self-caused and is the beginning of the laws of nature?"

Joe replied, "Yes. The universe, along with the laws of nature and physics, began simultaneously at the big bang."

"Doesn't it seem contradictory to say that the laws of physics began at the big bang event, when it takes the laws of physics to have produced

---

2. Briggs, "What Is the Big Bang?"
3. Ball, "Christian Physicist Examines," 24.
4. Hawking and Mlodinow, *Grand Design*, 83.

the big bang? How could the big bang happen without the laws of nature already in existence?" I argued that it is impossible that the law of physics created the laws of physics, just like it is impossible that I can be my own father. I could not have created myself.

Joe stopped to think on this and proposed that the laws of nature were *eternal*; they were *before* the big bang.

I asked, "But if the big bang was the beginning of time, and the laws of physics were *before* the big bang, then these laws had no beginning, so how could these laws start a process that led to the big bang?"

If someone states that these laws were eternal, then we get into the infinite regression argument again, which was refuted in chapter 6.

Nuclear physicist Gerald Schroeder shows that it is contradictory to argue for a quantum fluctuation as the cause of the universe. He writes: "Prior to the existence of the universe there was no nature and therefore there were no laws of quantum mechanics" to produce a "quantum fluctuation," and to say that the laws of nature were before the big bang "would suppose the existence of laws for a universe that does not exist."[5] It is contradictory to say that the laws of nature produced the laws of nature.

The Big Bang and Its Relationship to Time

The big bang theory asserts that this event was the cause of *space and time*. Frank Turek addresses the time problem by saying that it is contradictory to claim that in a God-less universe something happened before the big bang. This is because "there was no 'before' the Big Bang since there are no 'befores' without time, and there was no time until the Big Bang." Turek states that this idea of a moment prior to the big bang when space and time did not exist is "self-contradictory because it assumes time and space before there was time and space."[6]

The Claim That Physical Laws Came from Nothing

Physicist Victor Stenger suggests that scientific and mathematical theories show that "the universe appeared from an initial state in which there was

---

5. Schroeder, *Science of God*, 25.
6. Turek and Geisler, *I Don't Have Enough Faith*, 79–80.

The Option of a Self-Created Universe

no matter—from nothing.... So where did the laws of physics come from? They came from nothing!"[7]

Hawking writes: "Because there is a law like gravity, the universe can and will create itself from nothing," so "it is not necessary to invoke God" to explain the universe's existence.[8] John Lennox recognizes the contradiction of Hawking's statement by pointing out that "Hawking assumes that the law of gravity exists. [Gravity] is not nothing, so [Hawking] is guilty of a flat contradiction."[9]

Defining *Nothing*

When we begin with nothing (no *thing* whatsoever), J. P. Moreland says that we have to concede that this means "the complete and total lack of any being whatsoever."[10] Immanuel Kant says that if there is no existence of anything, it is "self-contradictory... that something is possible."[11]

Nothing plus nothing equals... nothing. If I have nothing in both hands and join them, I still have nothing. *Nothing* is like asking what my concrete driveway thinks about. The absence of any thing means no thing exists. *Nothing* lacks preference, because *nothing* does not possess the properties of mind or reason. *Nothing* does not have causal power to produce an effect.

Is Nothing, as a Cause, More Reasonable than God as a Cause?

What makes more sense: a spiritual Being created or *nothing* created? It is contradictory to believe that the cosmos came from the absence of anything. If it is said that belief in God is irrational, then how is the belief in *nothing as a cause* a more rational argument?

---

7. Stenger, *God: The Failed Hypothesis*, 130–31.
8. Hawking and Mlodinow, *Grand Design*, 180.
9. Lennox, *Can Science Explain Everything?*, 37.
10. Moreland, "Why Science Needs Philosophy," 551.
11. Kant, *One Possible Basis*, 79.

Sorting through Worldviews

Simple Examples to Illustrate the Need for a Personal Cause

A creation event needs a personal Being to do it. Chance and time do not provide this. Here are a few examples to show the need for a personal Beginner.

The circle and dot. During a lunchtime conversation, a co-worker said, "It's dumb to believe in God."

"Let me ask you something," I responded. I then took out a pen and placed a napkin the table. I drew a two-inch circle on the napkin and put a dot within the circle. I said, "Suppose this circle represents all possible knowledge—of medicine, physics, gardening, et cetera—and the dot represents all the knowledge that you know out of all possible knowledge."

He went along with this example.

I said, "Since you only know this small area of knowledge, the dotted area, how do you know that God is not out here [I pointed to the blank area in the circle] in an area that you know nothing about?"

"Maybe God is out there," he said.

I suggested that he was probably not an atheist. He was more of a *God-skeptic*—someone who admits he or she may not know, nor care, if there is a God, like having a God-apathy.

The spinning bin. A man gave me the argument that given enough time the universe could appear from nothing, by chance, and evolve over time (the chance plus time concept). I said, "It seems that you're saying that if I have a giant bin full of loose car parts from a dismantled Cadillac, and spin the bin for hundreds of billions of trillions of years, the Cadillac car will eventually come back together by pure chance."

He said, "Yes, theoretically, it could happen, given enough time."

"Okay," I said, "but let's start with a bin with nothing in it and spin it. Would this theoretical Cadillac car reassemble from chance plus time?"

A blank look was followed by "No."

It is unreasonable to say that nothing—the absence of any *thing*—has the power of production.

The coffee cup. A co-worker and I were in his office talking about whether God existed. My friend said, "The universe popped into existence from nothing."

"Are you saying that the universe was one-hundred percent empty, and then something popped into it?"

He said, "Yeah, sure, why not."

I asked him to pick up his empty coffee cup sitting on his desk and turn it over several times, which he did. "Astonishing, nothing came out,"

The Option of a Self-Created Universe

I said. I asked how long he would have to turn the cup over and over for something to come out. He said, "Probably forever, since it's empty."

I proposed that if his theory of an empty universe into which something popped into existence made sense, then it should also make sense to think that something will eventually come out of his empty coffee cup. But this is impossible, because emptiness cannot be a cause. Emptiness, without an outside influence, is still empty, no matter how much times passes.

The Unmoved Mover argument. Someone once said to me that the universe began when objects just popped into existence and moved against each other, then set off a cause-and-effect chain of events leading to today's state of the universe.

"Well, that's a theory I never heard of before," I said. "But let's go with that idea for a minute." So I asked, "Does it seem likely that in infinite empty space, impersonal objects would accidentally pop into existences that close together, then randomly collide and eventually produce the universe as it is today? And how did movement begin in empty space without any forces?"

"I don't know," he answered.

Medieval scholar St. Thomas Aquinas (b. 1225) says that this idea is impossible because it denies a first mover. Aquinas says it is evident that things are in motion, and what is in motion cannot move itself, so it must be moved by something already in motion. But this "cannot go on infinitely because then there would be no first mover." Aquinas says that something not moving has potential to move, but it cannot move from potential to actual unless it is moved by something actually moving. Aquinas correctly concludes that "it is necessary to arrive at a first mover which is moved by no other," and this we call God.[12]

The brain. An atheist told me that our brain developed by evolution, and we can now explain the origin of the universe without inserting a personal God as a cause for the universe.

I inquired: "Do you think that the origin of the universe is rooted in a reasonable and personal God, or are we rooted in a nonrational, accidental cause that is void of mind, purpose, and reason?"

"The universe began and evolved for no reason," he said.

"So evolution produced our brain?" I asked.

"Yes, to make a long story short," he said.

"You have discredited your own argument."

"How so?" he asked.

---

12. Aquinas, *Summa Theologica*, 12–13.

I explained it this way. "It is contradictory to insist that our origin is rooted in a self-caused universe that began for no reason, and that our brains evolved from a series of mindless collisions of molecules, and then say that our brains can give us an answer for our origin. The use of our brains to explain our origins is discredited by your theory."

C. S. Lewis expands this argument in *Miracles*, using a quote from another author who says it this way: "If my mental processes are determined wholly by the motions of atoms in my brain, I have no reason to suppose that my beliefs are true . . . and hence I have no reason for supposing my brain to be composed of atoms."[13]

A cause is either intelligent or not. To argue that our brain, which results from a nonintelligent and nonreasonable origin, can give us a reasonable and trustworthy explanation of our origin is an unreliable argument. The theory discredits our reason.

Laboratories Are Controlled Environments

When is it proposed that scientists in laboratories may one day replicate life and then claim that this shows no need for God, we might point out that these labs are, in fact, controlled environments created and occupied by intelligent scientists. The lab-producing-life argument only proves intelligence is behind life, not that life emerged from nonintelligence out of chaos. This lab argument proves more than it denies.[14]

Even Small Bangs Need a Cause

If there were no cause to the big bang, what about little bangs like from guns or firecrackers? No one thinks they're uncaused. Gregory Koukl says, "A big bang needs a Banger."[15]

It is contradictory to think that *nothing* was the cause for the beginning of the universe. It is contradictory to assert that the material universe created itself. A worldview that is contradictory must be false.

---

13. Lewis, *Miracles*, 22.
14. Tour, "Mystery of Origin of Life."
15. Koukl, "Tactics," 51.

Ingredients for a Cause Actually Show That God Exists

A *cause* that produces existence must have certain properties, such as power, intelligence, and desire. However, nothing—*no thing*—does not have power, or a reasonable mind, or a preference for creating instead of not creating. Everything that a *cause* needs sounds exactly like the Christian description of God's attributes. For the cosmos to begin, there must have been a mind that chose to create and had power to create. Only a personal Being can make these universal choices, because impersonal chance plus time has no predisposition to fill a void. The first cause must have been personal.

Conclusions So Far

Since there is no physical evidence of God's nonexistence, God cannot be disproved by science. Chapter 4 gave a list of four options for the existence of the universe. Option 1(a) was eliminated in chapter 5. Option 1(b) was eliminated in chapter 6. We have now eliminated option 2(a).

The next chapter will show that option 2(b) is the *most reasonable* conclusion of the four options: the universe began with a Creator.

8

The Option of a Divinely Created Universe
Either the Universe Had a Creator/God or It Did Not: Analyzing Option 2(b) from Chapter 4

There Are Not Multiple Gods as in New Age Philosophy

WHEN CHRISTIANS TALK ABOUT a divine Creator, we mean that there is only one such Being. This conflicts with some religious views that multiple gods exist. I'll begin the discussion on the biblical God as the Creator by first relating a story that shows the impossibility of polytheism—multiple gods. Polytheism is from the words *poly*, many, and *theos*, god.

At a work-related social gathering, a New Age[1] devotee told me that there are multiple gods in the cosmos. To begin my response I asked an initial question.

"Are these gods finite or infinite?"

She pursed her lips and said that they are probably finite.

"If so, then they have a beginning in space and time. Doesn't this imply an ultimate absolute, infinite, necessary Being who created them?"

"Maybe, but lesser gods connect us to the ultimate Being."

---

1. New Age philosophy with a polytheism connection can be seen at https://www.patheos.com/library/new-age/beliefs/ultimate-reality-and-divine-beings. Also see the second paragraph in the opening statement entitled "New Age Spirituality" at https://www.encyclopedia.com/religion/legal-and-political-magazines/new-age-spirituality, which states one of the features of New Age is "the innate divinity of all people."

"Let me ask you this. How can finite gods create the universe?"

She said, "Well, maybe they have infinite qualities."

"Like infinite existence, presence, power, and so forth?"

"Yes. The gods share identical attributes," she replied.

"But how can the universe have more than one infinite Being?" I suggested that the universe was not big enough to have multiple infinite gods, since the concept of infinite rules out the possibility of more than one; more than one ultimate Being is redundant. She had no response, so I went to my second question.

"Are the gods impersonal or personal?"

She said that she had not thought of this before but after a few seconds said, "Impersonal."

"Can you pray to these lesser gods, and will they respond?"

"Yes, in some way," she said.

"But how would impersonal gods prefer to answer prayers, since impersonal means without a preference? It sounds like the gods you're talking about are personal."

To my astonishment, she said that they might be personal.

Two contradictions result from her polytheism: (1) If multiple gods are *infinite and personal*, then they would share all of the possible characteristics of the others. Multiple infinite gods is redundancy. (2) If multiple gods are *finite*, then each is not what the other is, so these gods are distinctly different in attributes: one god is either better or worse than another. This makes it impossible to know if the god to whom a person is devoted is even a morally good god.

I suggested to her that she had a basic concept of the biblical God as infinite, personal, and plural in nature but that she had it convoluted in contradictory New Age and Eastern religious philosophy. I offered her the basic Christian Trinitarian concept of one God as the absolute, infinite, necessary Being, who is one in nature but three in persons. I affirmed to her that the Bible gives a noncontradictory concept of the nature of God that is not rationally objectionable.

We cannot reasonably hold the view that the universe was created by multiple gods, so let's move on to see that the beginning was caused by only one personal God.

If There Is a Starting Point, There Must Be a Starter

I was walking across the parking lot of my place of employment one afternoon when a co-worker, who knew I was a Christian, stopped me to say that he saw a TV science program about the big bang cosmic beginning. He was fascinated that the universe is expanding.

"Do you think that the universe expanded from a single point?" I asked.

"Yes, that's what the program said."

"Suppose we reversed the expanding process like we were hitting a remote's rewind button on a TV movie, would we eventually arrive at a single starting point?"

"Yes. Exactly!" he said.

"How did the starting point begin to expand?" I asked.

"God?"

"Yes. Exactly! A start implies a Starter," I said.

This began a conversation lasting several years after which my friend saw that the universe's first cause was God.

The x, y, z Example Shows That a First Cause Is Necessary

A friend and I were talking inside of a coffee shop about the origin of the universe. He said that there was no first cause; the universe has always existed; so God was unnecessary. I picked up a napkin and wrote "$a \ldots s, t, u, v, w, x, y, z$."

I explained my example. If z represents today, which came from y events, and y events came from x events, all the way back to a, then a is the start of existence for all subsequent events. If, for example, I eliminate t, then that eliminates every event subsequent to t; therefore, z, today, would never have arrived. Likewise, if we eliminate a—the first cause—then we eliminate all subsequent events; therefore, nothing would exist today. But we do exist, so there must be a first cause, and this is God.

Effects are the result of causes. If there is no first cause, then there are no subsequent events. But we do have events going on. It is contradictory to say that we exist in a series of cause-and-effects while simultaneously saying that there was no first cause to start the process. A contradictory theory is necessarily false.

The Option of a Divinely Created Universe

The Kalam Cosmological Argument

The term *kalam* (spelled various ways) derives from the Arabic word for speech.[2] A thousand years ago, Muslim theologians developed an argument to explain the cause of the universe, which has become known as the kalam cosmological argument.[3] *Cosmology* is a term pertaining to the cosmos: its origin, development, and arrangement. William Lane Craig summarizes the argument as follows.

- Whatever begins to exist has a cause.
- The universe began to exist.
- Therefore, the universe has a cause.[4]

Astronomer Hugh Ross writes: "If absolute nothingness spontaneously generates space, time, matter, and/or energy, then the principle of cause-and-effect has been violated. This would undermine the entire foundation of all the sciences, mathematics, and logic."[5]

Scientific knowledge is based on observing cause and effects. To say that the universe has no cause but itself is not a scientific statement; it's a philosophical one, because it presupposes that God does not exist.

What or Who Caused God?

The God-skeptic George Smith claims that the Christian argument that what exists must be caused is a contradictory idea. He thinks this because believers in God say "that everything must have a cause . . . . But if everything must have a cause, how did god become exempt?"[6] Smith is right about saying we are exempting God from having a cause. But why do we say that God is exempt? To answer this, we have to ask what the alternative concepts are if we do not exempt God from a cause. Two alternatives would be an infinite regression of events or an infinite regression of gods. In chapter 6, we saw that an infinite regression of any kind is impossible.

---

2. Kreeft and Tacelli, *Handbook of Christian Apologetics*, 58.
3. Groothuis, *Christian Apologetics*, 214.
4. Craig, "Cosmological Argument," 179–80.
5. Ross, *Creator and Cosmos*, 131.
6. G. H. Smith, *Atheism*, 239.

The kalam argument does not say *everything that exists* has a cause—only that which *began* to exist has a cause. It is impossible that God has a nature that can be caused. Why? First, it would imply an infinite regression of prior causes. Second, God's essence *is existence*. God is pure actuality. He does not have any potential to come into existence or become something else later.

Edward Feser says that to ask the question of what caused God is like asking "What caused the thing that cannot in principle have a cause?" and this amounts to asking a question that does not make sense.[7]

The Windowless Room

A man said to me, "I will not believe in God unless I see 100 percent evidence."

"Really? You would believe other things without absolutely 100 percent evidence, right?"

"Like what?"

I gave an example to him. Suppose you gave me a bucket of water and then placed me in a small windowless room. Then you closed and locked the only door and stood outside. One minute later you opened the door and saw that I was soaked, and the bucket was overturned. Would you believe me if I said someone else soaked me? No, you would not, even though you did not see the soaking event. Having 100 percent certainty is not necessary to believe I soaked myself. The evidence is enough. Juries, for example, vote guilty based on evidence of guilt "beyond reasonable doubt," not absolute certainty. We can reasonably conclude that the cosmos has a God without absolute, or 100 percent, certainty.

It is self-evident that the *Mona Lisa* had an intelligent painter; we are not justified in denying this. We *ought* to believe a personal painter exists, as a basic belief. W. Jay Wood says a belief is basic if "it is justifiably believed without the benefit of argumentative support, but no less reasonable for that."[8] Life's experiences show that we accept the existence of some object as coming from someone like a painter. We are justified in believing that the objects in the universe were created by a God who is intelligent and personal.

---

7. Feser, *Five Proofs*, 251.
8. Wood, *Epistemology*, 160.

The Option of a Divinely Created Universe

Some Reasons to Show a Divinely Created Universe

The following are some basic views to show that a personal God exists.

Intelligent design argument. The atheistic view is that the current form and order of the natural universe began without intelligent design or purpose and then evolved through chance collision of molecules. One of many intelligent design proponents is William Dembski, who writes: "For nature to be an object of inquiry for the scientist, nature must have an order which the scientist can grasp. If nature were totally without form and order, no science would be possible."[9] An atheistic scientist would not reasonably conclude that the form and order of sand castles came from random and unintelligent movements of wind and waves.

Messages imply intelligence. We reasonably conclude that circular patterns of leaves in a yard came from the accidental blowing of the wind. But if the leaves formed the sentence "Einstein was a brilliant scientist," we would naturally think there was an author, because there is a message—information—that cannot come by the chance blowing of the wind. Natural matter contains information such as DNA. Messages come from intelligence beyond material particles. The form and order of nature is a message of a Designer.

Laws of nature and mathematics. Scientists and mathematicians correctly interpret physical laws and principles of mathematical certainty as indications of form and order. But this implies that a *mind* is behind it all, not that order came about by *chance*, because chance is not a cause. Logic is a form of order. Peter Kreeft speaks of logic as that which "builds the mental habit of thinking in an orderly way."[10] Why would there be mental order today from a universe that began without a mind? Only a divinely caused universe with an orderly mind is the answer.

Sufficient cause argument. The view that the universe produced everything from *nothing* by chance implies that nothing—that is, no *thing*—is sufficient for creation. But a cause must possess what is sufficient to produce an effect. The sun, for example, must have what is sufficient to produce the effect of sunburn. Nothing is insufficient as a cause.

Living by the principle of sufficient reason. If it is argued that the entire universe of objects popped into existence, then why not think this happens all of the time? Why not think that a ten-pound rock will pop into existence

---

9. Dembski, *Intelligent Design*, 98.
10. Kreeft, *Socratic Logic*, 1.

and fall on your head? We don't believe this will happen, because it implies the rock created itself, and to create itself, it would have to precede itself, which makes no sense. There is sufficient reason to believe a Creator made the universe, because the universe stands as evidence of a Maker.

Apparent purpose argument. An exterminator told me that ants cooperate for the benefit of the colony's survival as their end goal. Aquinas says that if insects lack knowledge, then they must be directed towards their end by a Being with intelligence who knows the end goal. This Being is God.[11] Ants are still doing the same thing they have done for the past billion years. They have not progressed to develop ant condos. It appears that ants have one end goal, without their own knowledge, and this goal is from a mind who knows what the goal is.

Moral purpose and meaning. Humans have a sense of personal value, giving evidence that human life has meaning beyond mere naturalism. Humans act as if real moral right and wrong exist.[12] Scientist Frances Collins writes that there is something "peculiar" about human interaction regarding fairness and morals. He says that "the concept of right and wrong appears to be universal among all humans . . . approaching that of a law, like the law of gravitation."[13] This is how we know God is a Some-One, not a some-thing: God has preferences and relates to us as moral creatures.

Creation Is a Miracle

A skeptic once told me in words to this effect: "Belief in miracles is superstitious, because miracles mean that the laws of nature are violated, which is impossible."

I responded with an illustration. If I deposit five dollars into a box in my house each day for three days, the law of math tells me that I should have fifteen dollars. But suppose I have only ten dollars (because someone took five dollars on day 2). Was the law of math violated? No. A person merely tampered with the deposits. The law of math tells us what the amount will be, as long as the process is not tampered with. Since God created the laws of physics, he can override them without violating anything.[14]

---

11. Aquinas, *Summa Theologica*, 13.
12. Lewis, *Mere Christianity*, 3–8.
13. Collins, *Language of God*, 23.
14. Lewis, *God in the Dock*, 73.

The Option of a Divinely Created Universe

A supernatural event, to God, is natural to him. If we deny anything supernatural, we do not end up with just the natural; we end up with the unnatural idea that God doesn't do miracles.

Atheism Demands More Faith than a Christian Can Have

Faith in God, or faith in a God-less cause for the origin of the universe, requires the same thing: *faith*. The Christian believes by faith that our origin is rooted in God and considers evidence for a Creator as an aid to faith. The atheist, who has no evidence that God does not exist, wants us to believe on faith that the universe popped into existence out of nothing. Christians agree with apologist Frank Turek who says, "We don't have enough faith to be an atheist."[15]

Conclusions So Far

This chapter left us with God as the most reasonable explanation for the cause of the universe, in contrast to other options considered in previous chapters. But what kind of God are we talking about? Chapter 9 will explain that the biblical God as Trinity is theological, logical, and personally relevant.

---

15. Turek and Geisler, *I Don't Have Enough Faith*, 112.

9

The Trinity and the Deity of Christ
Living with Paradoxes in the Personal Nature of God

The Challenge of Defining the Biblical God

THE ARGUMENT FOR A God-caused universe was made in chapter 8, wherein God is seen as *personal*, which means that God has attributes distinct from impersonal nature. Now we will begin the challenging shift towards theological thinking about the nature of God as one God with a plural nature of three Persons. This is necessary if we want to speak to anyone about the biblical concept of God. The Christian concept of God is that he is a Trinity. This is the God whom we are now going to discuss.

The word *Trinity* is not used in the Old Testament (OT) or the New Testament (NT) to describe God's nature. The intent of OT narratives was not to overtly show God's Trinitarian nature. This changes when we read the NT, but the change is subtle. God's Trinitarian nature was assumed by Jesus's disciples who knew Christ personally. Because Christians in the first century spoke of Jesus as divine, it was necessary to assure people that Christians were still monotheistic (one God). Beginning in the second century, the church needed to define the Trinity doctrine to counter rising heresies. The doctrine was not invented, but the term Trinity was invented in order to explain the nature of God. Historian Bruce Shelley says that

Tertullian (d. AD 220) was a Latin-speaking church leader in North Africa and the first Christian to say that God was a *trinitas* (Latin for Trinity).[1]

Notice how Paul subtly weaves in the three Persons of the Trinity (Father, Son, and Spirit) into his Epistles to the Corinthians and to the Ephesians.

"May ... Jesus ... God ... Spirit be with you all" (2 Cor 13:14).

"For through him [the Son] we both have access to the Father by one Spirit" (Eph 2:18).

"I pray that ... he [the Father] ... through his Spirit ... so that Christ" (Eph 3:16–17).

"There is ... one Spirit ... one Lord [the Son] ... one God and Father" (Eph 4:4–7).

Paul's epistles were written before AD 68. This shows that the doctrine of the Trinity was believed by Christians early in the first century, and they did not need explanatory dissertations on the doctrine.

What the Trinity Is Definitely Not

Let's make clear what orthodox Christians state that the Trinity is *not*.

- *Not* tri-theism (three gods—from *tri*, three, and *theism*, god).
- *Not* polytheism (multiple gods).
- *Not* partitionism (the three persons are parts of God).
- *Not* subordinationism (the Son is inferior to the Father).
- *Not* 1+1+1=1, or 3=1 (this is mathematical nonsense).
- *Not* three gods in one God, or three persons in one Person, or three natures in one Nature. This is illogical, because if God is three gods, for example, then it is false that he is one God.

In a discussion with an anti-Trinitarian Jehovah's Witness, I asked the Witness, "What do you think I mean by the term Trinity?" He said it implied three gods, like a "committee." This committee idea made no sense to him. I agreed that it doesn't make sense, but this is because the Trinity is not a three-person committee debating, for example, on how to create the universe. Some anti-Trinitarians have an incorrect concept of what we mean by Trinity, then go about refuting a concept that we don't believe.

---

1. Shelley, *Church History*, 34.

Sorting through Worldviews

What the Trinity Definitely Is

The simplest defining phrase is that God is one in essence and three in persons. God is a plurality within a unity. In other words, there is only one God (monotheism, from *mono*, one, and *theism*, God), and this one God is a unity of three distinct persons, and the persons share the same nature—essence—of divinity. The Trinity is three distinct persons but not three *separate* persons. The Son, for example, cannot act independently or separately from the Father or the Spirit. God is not a composite of independent parts. Some definitions of the Trinity are given by notable Bible scholars.

- "The Father, the Son, and the Holy Spirit are all God"[2] (not three gods).
- The Trinity means a "threefold nature of God the Father, God the Son, and God the Holy Spirit."[3]
- "There is but one God," and "the one God is three—the Father . . . Son . . . Holy Spirit . . . constituting, the one divine essence."[4]

The Essence and the Persons of One God

An anti-Trinitarian Jehovah's Witness asked me, "Who was running the universe when God was in Mary's womb, if Jesus is God?" He confused the divinity of the Son with the Trinitarian God, as if Jesus were the Trinity. He did not make a distinction between God's essence and persons.

I explained that Christians are not saying that the Trinity became incarnate; only the Son became incarnate. Neither the Father nor the Spirit become incarnate, since this would imply that the Father or the Spirit died on the cross. But only the divine Son died on the cross. The distinction of persons helps us understand that Jesus was both divine and human.

The Trinity of Persons Are Not Identical Persons

There is one God, who is a tri-unity of distinct persons undivided in their divine nature. The unity of the persons does not mean they are identical

2. "Trinity," 1667.
3. Henry, "Trinity," 1625.
4. Grenz, *Theology for Community*, 66.

persons. Otto Weber says that "none of [the Bible's] statements asserts an identity between the Father and the Son. The Son is really the Son," not the Father or the Holy Spirit.[5] The Father, Son, and Spirit have identical divine natures without being identically the same person. This stands to reason, because three persons making one person is contradictory.

The Paradox of the Transrational Mystery in the Trinity

Anti-Trinitarians have told me that the doctrine "makes no rational sense." Of course it doesn't. This is because it is *transrational*. God exceeds what we can imagine. A discussion on God cannot fall under empirical and scientific analysis like analyzing a piece of fruit. It may seem counterintuitive to think of God as one God in three distinct persons, but the concept is not contradictory or rationally objectionable.

The Flatlander

Theologians Steven Boyer and Christopher Hall offer the following illustration to show the paradox that discussing God is "both reasonable and beyond reason."[6]

They propose a scenario of a two-dimensional person called a Flatlander, who sees only length and width, but not depth, and can give an exhausting geometrical analysis of a circle. But suppose another creature said that there is such a thing as a circle that extends upward: a cylinder, a three-dimensional object, one with depth. Boyer and Hall say that a Flatlander would have no concept of this "additional dimension," which to a Flatlander is "not easily susceptible of rational explanation" and therefore "a kind of mystery."[7] Boyer and Hall challenge us to think that something much more exists in our otherwise simply defined concept of God, and that the mystery that something more exists in God's nature is not irrational just because it is more than we imagine.

The concept of God as a Trinity emerged in the first century among Jews, Romans, and Greeks whose idea of a Trinitarian God was completely

---

5. Weber, *Foundations of Dogmatics*, 362.

6. Boyer and Hall, *Mystery of God*, 17. Olson uses the concept of Flatlanders in *Mosaic of Christian Belief*, 146.

7. Boyer and Hall, *Mystery of God*, 11.

outside of their religious worldview. So why would Christians propose the Trinity? Boyer and Hall point out that this is a good reason to take the doctrine of the Trinity seriously, because it is a doctrine that "no creature would ever have come up with on its own."[8] In other words, if Christians wanted Jews, Romans, and Greeks to believe in Jesus as a divine Messiah and Savior, then inventing a mythological Trinitarian doctrine was a very bad idea and would not have survived scrutiny.

The Ontological Nature of God

Ontology is the study of the "structure of reality."[9] According to *Webster's New World Thesaurus*, it is the study of "the nature of being." In other words, the ontological nature of something is what makes it what it is as opposed to something else. The ontology of granite means that its nature, or essence, is granite, not something else like plastic.

In regards to the Trinity, the ontological nature of the Father, Son, and Holy Spirit is the same: divine in all aspects of character and attributes. Fred Sanders says that the ontological view of the Trinity means "what God actually is."[10] It would be contradictory to define the Trinity by saying that the Father was divine in his nature, but the Son possesses a subordinate nature.

Contradictory and Unbiblical Examples of the Trinity

Representations from the physical world lead to false concepts of the Trinity. Christians cannot expect people to see the reasonableness of the doctrine if we give them logically flawed models. We don't want a Muslim to say, "If that's what you mean by the Trinity, then I reject it." The following are some illustrations that we should avoid using.

The Trinity is like an egg, three parts but one egg. The yolk contains more cholesterol than the white, so the ontology—nature—of the yolk is not the same as the white. This egg example contradicts the concept that the three persons of the Trinity share the same ontological nature.

The Trinity is like a three-leaf clover, three making one. The clover consists of a composite of parts that can be separated. But the persons of God

---

8. Boyer and Hall, *Mystery of God*, 115.
9. Lowe, "Ontology," 643.
10. Sanders, "What Trinitarian Theology Is For," 28.

are not a collection of separable parts. This clover example contradicts the tri-unity nature of the one God.

One man in three aspects: father, husband, employee. The man is *one* person—the *same* person—appearing in three modes. But the Trinity is *three* persons. This example contradicts the biblical concept that God is one but distinct in three persons.

Nature has parts, so nature is not a good model for the Trinity. Robert Letham says that God "is not divisible into parts. The three [persons] are not detachable, for they are each and together identical with the one indivisible being of God."[11]

The Deity of Christ Stated in the NT

Statements in the NT explicitly affirm the deity of Jesus, such as the following verses.

"The Word [the Son] was God" (John 1:1–2).

Thomas said to Jesus, "My Lord and my God" (John 20:28).

"Messiah [Christ] . . . is God" (Rom 9:5).

"For in Christ all the fullness of the Deity lives in bodily form" (Col 2:9).

Another way to state the deity of Christ is by Paul's statements that Christ the Son "*is* the image of God" (2 Cor 4:4 and Col 1:15), not that he was *made* in the image of God like all humans are made. Denying the deity of Jesus results in the nonsensical notion that what God's image is, is not God.

Hebrews 1:3 says that Jesus "is the radiance of God's glory and the exact representation of his of his being." Denying the deity of Jesus results in the contradictory idea that what the "exact representation" of God is, is not God.

Since God's image, or being, is divine, Jesus, as God's image and exact representative of God's being, is also eternally divine.

The Deity of Christ Seen by Connecting OT and NT Texts

Some OT texts referring to God (divinity) are used in the NT to apply explicitly to Jesus.

---

11. Letham, *Holy Trinity*, 188–89.

Sorting through Worldviews

Compare Isaiah 45:23 with Philippians 2:10–11 (knee to bow and tongue to swear/acknowledge). Isaiah speaks of the OT God, but Paul applies this to Jesus, thereby giving Jesus the same honor as God in the OT.

Joel 2:32 speaks of calling on the LORD God to be saved. But Paul, in Romans 10:9 and 13, applies this title to Jesus, thereby identifying Jesus of the NT with the same divinity as God in the OT. Dean Overman says that Paul was aware that the NT Greek term *kyrios* (Lord) "functioned as a substitute for the [OT] divine name of *Yahweh*."[12] (The name *Yahweh* is pronounced "yah-way.")

Compare Isaiah 44:6 with Revelation 22:13 (first and last). Isaiah speaks of the OT God, but John applies this to Jesus, thereby giving Jesus the same eternal attribute as God in the OT.

Verses in Revelation Applying Equally to Both God and Jesus

Revelation puts titles of God and Jesus in separate places. But to see that the titles as attributes of divinity apply to Jesus, we must see these texts together.

Observe the titles of God—divinity—in Revelation 1:8 and 21:6. Revelation 1:8 says, "I [God] am . . . Alpha and . . . Omega" (the first and last letters of the Greek alphabet). Revelation 21:6 says, "I [God] am . . . Alpha and . . . Omega, the Beginning and . . . End." But Revelation 22:13 applies these terms to Jesus, thereby showing that Jesus has the same attributes as God.

Mark Wilson states that Alpha and Omega used in Revelation 1:8; 21:6; and 22:13 "are examples of *merism*—a figure of speech that combines two contrasting words to refer to an entirety, in this case the eternal nature of the God of all time."[13]

Logically, how many *beginnings* or *firsts* can there be? The terms are synonymous, and divinity applies equally to God the Father and to Jesus the Son.

---

12. Overman, *Case for Divinity of Jesus*, 24.
13. Wilson, "Revelation," 1302.

The Trinity and the Deity of Christ

Why Didn't Jesus Just Plainly State That He Was God?

If Jesus had declared "I'm God!" people could have walked away thinking they had sufficient information to satisfy their intellectual curiosity. Instead, Jesus's parables, for example, are intended to draw people into the stories to experience God rather than to satisfy our quest to solve a mystery. Jesus wants us to have a relationship with God, not mere rational information about God. Maybe this is why Jesus never wrote a book.

NT Texts Showing the Personal Nature of the Holy Spirit

The Jehovah's Witnesses maintain that the Holy Spirit is an impersonal force in a succinct statement: the Spirit is "not a person but is God's active force by which he accomplishes his purpose and executes his will."[14] In the Jehovah's Witness website under "What Do Jehovah's Witnesses Believe?" fifteen topics are listed in bold print.[15] The Holy Spirit is not one of the topics. Why? Maybe because inquiring people with a biblical church background would be shocked to know the Witnesses deny the personhood and divinity of the Holy Spirit.

An impersonal force, like electricity, would not have personal, intellectual, and moral attributes as the following examples show regarding the Holy Spirit.

An impersonal force without a mind cannot distinguish truth from error, but the Holy Spirit can:

"But . . . the Spirit . . . will teach you" (John 14:26).

"The Spirit of truth . . . will testify" (John 15:26).

An impersonal force does not possess emotions or feelings, but the Holy Spirit does:

"God's love . . . through the . . . Holy Spirit" (Rom 5:5).

"For the kingdom of God is . . . joy in the Holy Spirit" (Rom 14:17).

"And do not grieve the Holy Spirit of God" (Eph 4:30).

An impersonal force cannot speak a preference to lead one way or the other, but the Holy Spirit can:

"While they were worshiping . . . the Holy Spirit said" (Acts 13:2).

"For if you . . . are led by the Spirit of God" (Rom 8:13–14).

---

14. "Spirit," in *Insight on the Scriptures*, 1019.
15. https://www.jw.org/en/jehovahs-witnesses/faq/jehovah-witness-beliefs.

An impersonal force cannot be lied to or spoken against, but you can do this to the Holy Spirit:

"Then Peter said . . . you have lied to the Holy Spirit" (Acts 5:3).

"But . . . speaks against the Holy Spirit" (Matt 12:31).

The "Another" in John 14 and 15 Cannot Be Impersonal

Notice the word *advocate* in John 14 and 15. In John 14:16–17, Jesus says that after he leaves his disciples, the Father will send "another advocate to help you . . . the Spirit of truth." In John 14:26, Jesus adds, "The Advocate, the Holy Spirit . . . will teach you . . . and remind you of everything I have said to you." In John 15:26, Jesus rephrases and says, "When the Advocate comes, whom I will send to you . . . the Spirit of truth . . . he will testify about me."

The Jehovah's Witnesses' New World Translation of the Bible uses "helper" instead of "Advocate," and so does the English Standard Version. The Greek word here is *paraklētos*. Greek scholar Gerhard Kittle says that this word "seems to have the broad and general sense of 'helper.'"[16]

Jesus says he would not send himself; instead, he would send "another." But Jesus is personal. If the Holy Spirit is an impersonal force, then the Spirit cannot be another, and therefore the word another is meaningless.

Along this line, in Acts 1:8, Jesus tells his group of disciples that they would receive "power when the Holy Spirit comes on" them. Dale Brunner writes that "Jesus himself is the subject of the Spirit's work in history," and Luke, the author of Acts, "wishes here . . . to connect the work of Jesus with the ministry of the Spirit," so we would see that what the Spirit does is not a separate work from Jesus.[17]

This makes sense if the another whom Jesus sends is personal; otherwise, we would have the contradictory idea that Jesus's personal work is later enhanced by an impersonal force.

The Spirit Is Associated with the Father and Son

Jesus directed his disciples to "go" into the world and teach and baptize in the "name of the Father . . . Son . . . and . . . Spirit" (Matt 28:19–20). If the

---

16. Kittle and Friedrich, *Theological Dictionary*, 5:804.
17. F. Brunner, *Theology of Holy Spirit*, 156.

Spirit is impersonal, then why is he named with the persons of Father and Son and included in the command to go in their *singular* name and not in plural names? The singular use of name shows the divine unity of the persons. The Spirit is in the divine Trinitarian community of God. The persons of the Trinity reveal each other, but as one God, or one name.

The Relevance of Community Is Shown in the Trinity

The three persons of the Trinity show God as an eternal personal community.[18] The doctrine of the Trinity explains why humans crave loving social interaction in an organized community. It may be argued by the atheist that society is for survival—to pass on our genes. However, in societies, we have events such as art exhibits, concerts, stand-up comedy routines, sports, community fireworks; but none of these things have anything to do with survival in a purely materialistic world. The Trinity is relevant in our everyday life.

The Paradox of Theology

This chapter attempted to simplify a complicated doctrine by citing a few references to Scripture texts and theological concepts. Brunner advises us that theology is a way of "keeping the gospel from becoming complex," and paradoxically, it is also the "science of keeping the gospel" from becoming too simple.[19] Our mind hosts various ideas about God, not all of which are correct. The Bible gives us insights that need to percolate in our minds, so that we can explain them to others without apology. Christians should not make an apology for theology.

Moving from Doctrine to Conversation

The doctrine of the Trinity is directly related to conversations with anyone who has a religious view, especially Jehovah's Witnesses, Mormons, Muslims, and Jews. We will see how this plays out in the next four chapters.

---

18. Torrance, *Christian Doctrine of God*, 62.
19. F. Brunner, *Holy Spirit*, 25.

10

Jehovah's Witnesses

Their View of Christ and Maintaining a Meaningful Dialogue

Watch Tower

THE WATCH TOWER BIBLE and Tract Society of Pennsylvania is the Jehovah's Witnesses nonprofit organization. They have their own Bible translation called the New World Translation of the Holy Scriptures (NWT), which was introduced in chapter 9. Their two major magazines are *Awake!* and *The Watchtower*. Their place of worship is called a Kingdom Hall, not a church building, as in traditional Christianity.[1]

Strong Resistance to the Trinity at Your Front Door

When two Jehovah's Witnesses knock at your front door, they are there to convert you to their religious movement and away from any Trinitarian concept of God you may have. Their organization is staunchly anti-Trinitarian. That is why I discuss this movement immediately after the chapter on the Trinity. I will highlight a few primary doctrines of the Witnesses to help us have a calm and reasonable discussion with them about the nature of God, Jesus, and the Holy Spirit, using the method of asking questions.

---

1. See https://www.jw.org for further details.

All Witnesses I have met and know personally are very fine people. This chapter is not a personal criticism of any Witness, just a critique of their doctrinal views.

The Initial Meeting at the Front Door and the Holy Spirit

On a Saturday morning while seated in my living room, I heard three knocks on the front door. They were timid ones, not like a cop's knock. I recognized the cadence: Jehovah's Witnesses. I opened the door for a chat with two men. We talked in general about God before I asked them to tell me about the nature of God. They did not know what I was asking, so I explained that I would like to know what the word God meant. What was the essence or moral substance of God? What attributes constituted God's nature as God?

One man replied that God—Jehovah—was a Spirit who created the universe. I asked about the nature of Jesus. He said that Jesus was God's first creation, the Son of God, but not divine. I asked about the nature of the Holy Spirit. He said that the Spirit is a term to explain God's use of power as a force. (Jehovah's Witnesses publications claim that the Holy Spirit "is not a Person" but, instead, is an "impersonal" force.[2])

I asked, "Are you saying that the term 'Holy Spirit' is only an explanation of God's power, but the Spirit is not divine?"

He said, "Yes."

"Is this force *personal* or *impersonal*, like electricity that powers machines, is impersonal?"

He said that the Holy Spirit was like impersonal electricity.

"Watch this," I said. I raised one arm to shoulder height and then lowered it.

"Let me ask you this. Is the power that moved my arm an impersonal force outside of my body that came upon me?"

He said, "No."

I then posed this concept: since the power that raised my arms came from *me*, the power must be personal, because I am personal. Similarly, the Spirit must have the personal divine nature as God if the Spirit is God's power.

I finished our conversation, suggesting to him to look through a Bible concordance for all of the NT entries for Holy Spirit or Spirit and read

---

2. "Spirit," in *Insight on the Scriptures*, 1019–20.

the corresponding biblical texts. I proposed that it would be impossible to conclude that the Spirit was an impersonal force after doing this.

The personal nature of the Holy Spirit can be seen in the following story.

The Holy Spirit as One Who Comforts

I have a friendship with a married couple who are Jehovah's Witnesses. In an office cafeteria one day, we were discussing religious views and how God provides comfort to people. I asked them about their concept of the nature of the Holy Spirit.

The man said that the Spirit is the "power God uses when he does something."

"The Holy Spirit is like a force then?"

"Yes," they both said.

I pointed to an adjacent refrigerator and asked if this force was like the electricity that powered the refrigerator.

They said that this was a good example of the Holy Spirit as power.

"Is the Holy Spirit a *personal* or an *impersonal* force?" I asked.

They looked at each other and back at me, and then the man said that the Spirit was an impersonal force, not a person like God the Father.

"That's interesting," I said. "Let me ask you a few questions." I posed three questions.

"How does an impersonal force like electricity have the moral characteristic of being 'holy'?" Neither one had an answer.

"How can an impersonal electrical force offer comfort?" I gestured to the refrigerator and asked if it seemed likely that someone would sit next to it if one needed comfort. They agreed that this was unlikely.

"How would an impersonal force, with no intellect, even know someone needed comfort?" They told me that they didn't know.

I referenced John 14:16. This states that the Holy Spirit is an Advocate, like a Counselor (the Jehovah's Witness NWT says "helper"). I asked them how an impersonal force could have the comforting or helping nature of a person while being an impersonal force. I mentioned that Jesus said he was leaving his disciples, but would send another comforter to them. I asked, "What benefit would it be to the disciples if Jesus, who was a personal helper, sent another comforter that is impersonal?" I asked if this sounds like the Spirit qualifies as "another."

As they quietly thought on this, I referred them to Matthew 1:20. Matthew says, regarding the coming birth of Jesus, that "what is conceived in her [Mary] is from the Holy Spirit." I asked, "How can an impersonal force produce a person?" I drew the conclusion that if the Spirit is impersonal, then this implies that Jesus was half personal from Mary and half impersonal from the Spirit. I asked them if that made sense. They looked at each other, shrugged, and said that they had never thought of any of this before. I have had several conversations with this couple over the years, but they are still Jehovah's Witnesses.

The previous chapter 9 shows biblical texts on the personal nature of the Spirit.

God the Father Is a Loving Father from Eternity

Two Jehovah's Witnesses came to my door recently. I invited them to come inside. We sat in my study and talked together. I asked them for their doctrinal view of the nature of God the Father, Jesus, and the Holy Spirit. I received the basic Witness view: one eternal God the Father; Jesus the non-divine and created son; and the Spirit the active force of God, but not personal.

"Jesus was created in space and time?" I asked.

"Yes," one man said and referenced Colossians 1:15. He told me this verse showed that "Jesus was God's first creation."

"Does this mean that prior to Jesus's creation, God was an eternal lone entity?" To clarify, I defined lone entity to mean that God was a lone Being—not a plural unity of three persons as in the Trinity.

They said that this was their view.

We opened the Bible to 1 John 4:8 and read that "God is love."

"Let me ask you this. Isn't love a relationship between someone to love and someone to return love? If God is a lone person, how could God possess love from eternity without relationship?"

There was no response, so I said, "I think I have a solution to this dilemma: God created a moral being, Jesus, so then God began a loving relationship."

They looked at each other and conceded that this was a solution.

"Well, I think we have an even bigger and contradictory problem if you claim this," I said. I explained that if we say God the Father had to create a moral being to have relationship, this implied that God's moral nature changed in time: at one time God was not love but became love. How could an eternal God undergo a moral change in time? God does not become better over time. God is the ground of his own being, so all attributes of God are eternal. Therefore, the Son must be as eternal as the Father. The Son must be divine.

I proposed that if God created the Son, then there was a time when no Son existed. Therefore, there was a time when God's attribute as a Father did not exist either. Logically, this means God became a Father, in time. This idea of a changeable nature of God is contrary to Psalm 90:2, which states that God is "from everlasting to everlasting." To be from everlasting means to dwell in a realm in which there was no time. Therefore, for God's nature to change in time is contradictory. When talking with Jehovah's Witness, we must think through their propositions to see them as contradictions to the nature of God.

Can God Die?

A Jehovah's Witness attempted to refute the deity of Christ by proposing the following argument to me.

"Can God die?" he asked. I said no. "Did Jesus die?" I said yes, he did. "Then Jesus can't be God," he concluded.

That God cannot die is true only if we're talking about God in his nature as Trinity. God the Trinity cannot die, but the divine Son, who became a human, could and did die. The Son was incarnate, not the Trinity. Jesus, formerly in the nature of God, took on human nature, and could suffer and die.[3] The Witnesses miss the concept that, as a human, Jesus was subject to death, like all humans.

He moved on to say that John 14:28 proves that Jesus is inferior to God when Jesus says that "the Father is greater than I." But note his misreading of this text. Jesus says that the Father is greater, not better or qualitatively superior to him. In the context of the story, starting at verse 1, Jesus is talking about how the Father originates the coming of the Holy Spirit. Jesus is not making a claim that the Father is qualitatively superior. John 14:28 was true during the time Jesus was a human.

---

3. Philippians 2:6 (NIV) states that Christ was "in very nature [form] God" and had "equality with God" but did not hold on to this and took instead "the very nature [form] of a servant." The ESV uses "form." The Son became a human but retained divinity.

The Son Is Timelessly Begotten

Two elderly gentlemen came to my house announcing that they were Jehovah's Witnesses and wanted to talk. I suggested that they return in a couple days for a more casual conversation. They returned two nights later for a two-and-a-half-hour discussion in my home.

John 3:16 came up in the conversation. Their NWT states that Jesus was the "only-begotten Son" of God. They concluded that because Jesus was begotten, then he came into existence in space and time, similar to a human father who begets a child.

I asked, "Are you saying that the Son, as 'begotten,' means that the eternal Father *caused* the Son to exist; the Son is an effect in time? Therefore, the Son is not divine, nor co-equal with God?"

They said, "Yes, because 'begotten' shows God caused Jesus to exist."

I pointed out that Jesus was "begotten," not "made" by the Father. I explained that human fathers *beget* human beings with a nature like themselves. However, human beings *make* things like chairs or bridges; things that are completely unlike themselves.[4] Their NWT of John 3:16 says that God gave his *begotten* Son, not his *created* Son. The NWT actually affirms that the Son has the same nature as God by the use of begotten.

Jesus as the Firstborn Means Preeminence

Another overly literalistic mistake is made by the Jehovah's Witnesses in Colossians 1, as the following conversation will show.

I asked these two men, "Can you tell me where else in the Bible you believe it says that the Son was created?"

They turned to Paul's letter to the Colossians in their NWT and read where it says that Jesus is "the firstborn of all creation" (Col 1:15–16). They explained that "firstborn of all creation" means that he was the *first thing God created.*

"Are you saying that 'firstborn' means 'first thing created' in chronological time sequence'?" I asked. They said yes. I asked, "Do you realize that this view totally ignores what the term 'firstborn' meant to Paul, and other ancient Jews in their culture?" They asked me what I meant.

I directed their attention to Genesis 41:51–52, where it states that Joseph had two literal sons in this chronological space/time order: Manasseh,

---

4. This concept is from Lewis, *Mere Christianity*, 153–59.

the "firstborn," and Ephraim, the "second son." In Israel's ancient culture, a firstborn son was the preeminent one in the family and received the main portion of inheritance. This would be Manasseh's firstborn right.

However, in Genesis 48:12–20, the term firstborn is used differently. Joseph's father, Israel (formerly called Jacob), prays for his grandsons, Manasseh and Ephraim. Israel places "his right hand... on Ephraim's head" (v. 14) with the result that Israel "put Ephraim ahead of Manasseh" (v. 20). Ephraim is placed in the *firstborn status* of preeminence, even though literally the second born.

I also turned to Jeremiah 31:9, which provides an example of how firstborn is used as preeminence instead of as physically literal. In this text, Ephraim is used synonymously for Israel: "Ephraim is my firstborn son." This shows ancient Israel's status as preeminent among the nations and demonstrates that the term firstborn does not always mean first in chronological time sequence in Jewish tradition.

I referred these two men back to Colossians 1. According to their interpretation of firstborn, it means first in *chronological order* in space and time. If so, then verse 18, which says in their NWT that Jesus was "the firstborn from the dead," should mean that he was first person chronologically who was raised from the dead. That is, we could read verses 15 and 18 like this: Jesus was "the firstborn [first one in chronological order] of all creation" (v. 15); and Jesus was "the firstborn [first one in chronological order] from the dead" (v. 18).

Logically, if firstborn in verse 15 means chronological time, then firstborn in verse 18 means the same thing. But it is not true that Jesus was the first person in chronological time to be raised from the dead (Jesus raised Lazarus, as told in John 11). Therefore, the term firstborn in verses 15 and 18 cannot have anything to do with chronological time. Instead, it has everything to do with Jesus as *preeminent*, in accordance with how ancient Jews viewed the firstborn status.

Lastly, I read Colossians 1:15–18 out loud. Verse 18 says that by Jesus's resurrection, Jesus became "first in all things" (NWT). The NIV says that "he might have the supremacy" resulting from the resurrection. In other words, no matter what translation we read, firstborn has to do with Jesus being first in status or preeminence, not first in physical chronology.

In a comment on Colossians 1:15, David Pao writes that firstborn can "be used in a metaphorical sense where rank rather than temporal priority" is meant.[5]

G. K. Beale writes that firstborn in Colossians 1:15 indicates that Christ was not the "beginning part of the creation" but refers to the eternal nature of the Son, "which places Christ as separate from the rest of creation," because verses 16 and 17 state that the Son created all things.[6]

The Jehovah's Witnesses use of Colossians 1:15 in the twenty-first century completely bypasses the ancient Jewish cultural and theological use of the term *firstborn*.

Photons at the Front Door

A Jehovah's Witness team of two came to my house one midmorning. I stepped outside with my Bible for a chat. (How great is this: people coming to our door to hear about Jesus.) Eventually I asked, "Does Jesus share the same divine nature as God the Father?"

They said, "No. He is inferior, because he was created."

I pointed up to the sky and said, "Look over there to the sun." I asked if the photons coming from the sun were actually the sun or whether the photons were an inferior substance that came into existence while on the way to Earth.

They said: "The same substance."

I said that since we agree that the photons *are* the sun, and not something else, it would be contradictory to assert that what the sun radiates, as photons, is not the sun. They agreed.

At this point I opened my Bible to Hebrews 1:3. This says that Jesus "is the radiance of God's glory and the exact representation of his being."

I proposed some questions. If the Son Jesus does not have the same divine nature as God, then how is it possible for the Son to radiate God's glory and be the "exact representation of his being"? Wouldn't that be like saying that what God radiates is not God? In other words, I explained, we all agreed that the photons radiating from the sun are, in fact, the sun and that it is contradictory to say that what the sun radiates, as photons, is not the sun. Following this reasoning, if we claim that what God radiates is not

---

5. Pao, *Colossians and Philemon*, 95.
6. Beale, "Colossians," 854.

divine, we might just as well argue that what the sun radiates is not the sun. But this is contradictory.

Their rebuttal was to show me their NWT that says that the Son was not the "radiance" of God's glory but the "reflection" of God's glory. But this makes no difference because of the context of Hebrews 1:1–3. I proposed that their view that the Son, as a non-divine reflection of God, produces this contradiction: what God reflects from his nature is not divine. In either case, the Jehovah's Witness view of Jesus is logically contrary to the core of the nature of Jesus in these three verses.

If Jesus is not the divine self-revelation of God, then humans are still without a true revelation of God. If that is the case, then humans are left to themselves to figure out the nature of God. The Jehovah's Witness theology leaves us no clear revelation of God.

Jesus Is Not a Little God in John 1:1

The discussion continued to John 1:1–2 from which I made various observations and comments.[7] All major translations have similar wording as in the NIV.

The text reads as follows. Verse 1 says, "In the beginning was the Word, and the Word was with God, and the Word was God." And verse 2 says, "He was in the beginning with God."

In this context, the Word and Jesus are synonymous. The NWT, however, changes the end phrase of verse 1 to this: "the Word was *a god* [emphasis added]." I asked if this phrase "a god" means that Jesus does not have the divine nature of God. They said that Jesus is not divine and began Scripture quoting. I listened for a moment, then said, "That's very interesting. But let me ask you something. Did the Word, meaning Jesus, begin in space and time?" They said "Yes, because the Son was the first creative act of God."

This statement corresponds to their literature that says Jesus was "the beginning of Jehovah's creative works . . . God's first creation."[8] If that is the case, then space and time began with this first creative act, because before anything was created there was only eternity. Eternity is the realm of divinity; space and time is the realm of non-divinity—of things created.

I asked, "Was there a time in which God began to exist?"

---

7. These thoughts were inspired by comments from Barth, *Church Dogmatics*, II/2:94–102.

8. "Jesus Christ," in *Insight on the Scriptures*, 52.

They said, "No."

We concluded that God has no relationship with a beginning in space and time, so this places God in eternity, a divine realm.[9] Pressing on, I pointed out that the text says that the Word was "in the beginning" and that the Word was "with God." When was the Word with God? Well, *in the beginning*. Therefore, I inquired, how is it possible that the Word could have been "in the beginning" and be "with God," *in the beginning*, if the Word itself had a beginning?

No answer was proposed. I said, "Let's look at the text." I pointed out that we agreed that God has no beginning. But the Word was there with God *before* there was a beginning. This is eternity, the divine realm. The text is saying that whatever relationship God has with a beginning (which is none), so does the Word. Or to restate: God has no beginning, and neither does the Word. Therefore, the Word must share divine nature, because only God is without a beginning. Concluding John 1:1 with "a god" is contradictory to what precedes this phrase in the same verse.

Note that John 1:1 does *not* say that the Word had a beginning, nor that the Word began to exist, nor that the Word was created. It does say, however, that the Word was in the beginning and "did not arise later."[10]

Furthermore, John 1:1 does not begin with the phrase "In the beginning was *a word*." The phrase "the Word" contradicts their phrase "a god." If the Word is just "a god," then John would have said, "In the beginning was *a word* . . . and the word was *a god*." The Watch Tower's term "a god" is motivated by their doctrinal position rather than by a consistent view of the nature of Jesus in the context of verse 1.

Jesus Is Not a Created Thing, Because He Created All Things

Our discussion went to John 1:3. I drew two boxes on a piece of paper to show that there are only two categories of existence in the universe:

Uncreated Existence	*Created Existence/Created Things*
(divinity/God)	(all else/non-God)

---

9. This thought was prompted by Ayers, "As We Are One," 108.
10. Ayers, "As We Are One," 95.

In which category does Jesus belong? If in the category of created things, then what do we do with verse 3 that says, "Through him all things were made, without him nothing was made that has been made." It is a contradiction to assert that Jesus made all things yet is one of the things made, because this implies that Jesus created himself, which is impossible. Moreover, Colossians 1:17 states that Jesus "is *before* all things [emphasis added]." It is impossible that Jesus could be before all things and also be one of the things. Therefore, the only remaining category is the divine category of an uncreated Being: God.

The Witnesses' idea of Jesus contradicts John 1:1–3. Whatever concept of the Witnesses' doctrine results in a contradiction is false by necessity: it is not possibly false, it is not false on Earth but true in the Andromeda Galaxy, it is not false today but true tomorrow. What contradicts is false universally.

The Implications if the Deity of Christ Is Denied

The religious doctrinal views of the Jehovah's Witnesses about Jesus Christ result in a view of Christ like the following.

- He is a finite creation in space and time, like all created humans.
- He is a work of God, unable to redeem failed human works.
- His death was insufficient for universal salvation.
- Jesus is an insufficient revelation of God.
- God did not enter humanity, so God is still separate from us.

The Importance of Reading Books by Biblical Scholars

In AD 325, the Council of Nicaea rejected the doctrine of a created Jesus in favor of the full divinity of Christ.[11] Any book on church history will tell you this. It is important for Christians to read scholarly books.

I conclude conversations with Jehovah's Witness by asking, "Can you tell me the name of a couple of your favorite theologians whose books have educated and inspired you?" Witnesses always tell me that they only read publications of their own organization. I suggest that this presents a

---

11. Hill, *History of Christian Thought*, 61.

narrow worldview of Christianity. I tell them that there are many popular authors who would give them an introduction to basic biblical Christianity, and I write down on a piece of paper two names: Timothy Keller and Philip Yancey.

11

Mormons

Their Religious System and Staying on Track in a Dialogue

Discussions with Mormons Moves Us into Another Realm

THE PREVIOUS CHAPTER ON how to talk with Jehovah's Witnesses was straightforward, since their main doctrine was the denial of the Trinity; discussions with them was confined to this topic. This is not the case when talking with Mormons. Mormonism claims to be Trinitarian. But Mormonism has redefined the concept of the persons of God and Jesus and also redefined the doctrine of the Trinity to be unlike the biblical and historical Christian doctrines. This chapter critiques Mormonism's doctrine of God, to show it is not in the biblical realm.

The Reason That Mormons Are at Your Front Door

Mormons have a commendable commitment to morals and family. Conversations with the Mormons are pleasant, because Mormons are kind and respectful. But when Mormons are at your front door, they are there to convey the message that their religious doctrinal system is the culmination of all spiritual truth through Joseph Smith (1804–1844) and Smith's successors and that *The Book of Mormon* is the means to know this truth.

You do not need to know details of their doctrines in order to have a simple and nonconfrontational conversation with Mormon visitors. Just ask some initial questions, then follow the implications of their answers with basic commonsense reasoning.

Clarity of Terms and Publications

The official name of this religion is The Church of Jesus Christ of Latter-Day Saints. Their headquarters is located in Salt Lake City, Utah. The designation *Mormon* comes from a person who had this name in *The Book of Mormon* (Mormon 1:1). I will use the terms Mormon or Mormonism as synonymous to their official name. Joseph Smith is *the* prophet, founder, and first president of the Mormon Church. The Mormon Church claims divine revelation for these four publications: (1) *The Book of Mormon*, (2) *Doctrine and Covenants*,[1] (3) *The Pearl of Great Price*, (4) and the Bible, which predates the first three books.

Mormonism holds to the concept of *progressive revelation*. This means that new doctrinal views came after the Bible, and these views are inspired by God, even if the new revelation contradicts the Bible. This implies that the Bible is subordinate to Mormon publications.

Biblical Christians also speak of progressive revelation. For example, the NT reveals more than the OT reveals. But in contrast to the Mormon idea, biblical Christians do not believe that revelation put into a book subsequent to the Bible is equally inspired. With the completion of the Bible, divinely inspired books ceased. For a biblical Christian, progressive revelation means that biblical truth can be expounded upon for personal and doctrinal insights. Biblical Christians believe interpretations of the Bible are true if the interpretation coincides with the Bible; contradictions to the Bible are rejected as false. But for Mormons, the Bible is interpreted correctly only if the interpretation coincides with Mormon doctrine.

The position of elder is the introductory position for any *man* who wants to advance in the Mormon Church's hierarchy. Any man or woman representing the Mormon Church is considered a *missionary* for their

---

1. See G. A. Smith, *Doctrine of Covenants*. The title page of *Doctrine of Covenants* states that the book is "Containing Revelations Given to Joseph Smith, the Prophet." The title page of *The Pearl of Great Price* states that it is "a selection from the revelations . . . of Joseph Smith."

cause. A local congregation is called a ward, in contrast to a church, as in traditional Christianity.

Two Questions to Ask at the Beginning of a Conversation

To avoid anxiety when Mormons arrive at your front door, just ask questions. Begin with: "Can you tell me about the nature of God?" With practiced panache, their answer will sound biblical: God created the universe, loves us, and so on. But the term *God* needs to be defined in your conversation. Hold that thought. Go to a second question: "How did the Mormon Church movement begin?" This will begin to unfold their definition of God.

The following are some recaps of conversations I have had with Mormons, which are given to show how to bring their concept of God into the open. Also, these examples will show that the Mormon concept of God is contradictory to the Bible.

The Mormon God Has a Physical Body on Kolob

Two young ladies, Ms. Jones and Ms. Clark (not their real names), from the local Mormon ward, came to my front door one recent Saturday morning. Here is how the conversation about God developed.

Their introductory comments included asking me if I knew anything about the Mormon Church. I said that I knew some things, but I did have some questions, and I immediately asked, "Can you tell me what the Mormon concept of God is: what is God's nature?"

Their first response was that God is the Father of us and loves us, and he is the Father of the Son, Jesus.

"How did the Mormon Church begin?" I asked.

Ms. Jones said that it started about 1820, when God the Father and Jesus stood before Joseph Smith, announcing to Smith that he was to receive the truth of Christianity. Notice that her answer implied that God was in a physical body.

I asked: "Were the Father and Jesus there physically?"

She explained that God and the Son have a body of "flesh and bones."[2]

"This implies that God and Jesus occupy a location in space. Do you know where this location is?" I asked.

---

2. G. A. Smith, *Doctrine and Covenants* 130:22, explicitly says this.

Both women said that they did not know.

I politely ventured on. "Let me ask you this. Based on God having a body, does it seem reasonable to conclude that God must be on a physical planet like humans are on planet Earth?"

Ms. Jones said that there is a concept in Mormonism of Kolob as the unknown location where God lives.[3] Her answer coincides with Mormon author Bruce McConkie's description of Kolob, which he gleaned from The Book of Abraham, as "the planet 'nearest to the celestial, or the residence of God.'"[4]

I asked if they could show me anything in the Bible about God having a physical body. Instead of showing me texts, they verbally referenced biblical passages that say God has hands and arms, which indicates he has body parts. I agreed that the Bible uses these terms, but should we conclude that God is a bird because Psalm 91:4 says that God covers us "with his feathers" and "wings"? Note that they interpreted texts about hands and arms of God in accordance with Mormonism's theology, thereby ignoring biblical use of metaphors and other poetic literary styles.

We read John 4:24, which states "God is spirit." "How is it possible," I asked, "that God is simultaneously a nonphysical spirit and a physical body on a planet? Didn't this seem contradictory?" The women did not have an answer to this contradiction.

In three minutes we have learned, by asking questions, that the God of Mormonism resides in a body in a location of space, and we have not actually *told* them anything yet. Let's move on.

The Mormon Idea That God Became the God over Us

Ms. Clark interjected that all of this talk about God's nature is speculation. Instead, we should try to get to know God and, eventually, through an "exaltation" process, become gods.

"Are you saying that God became God, and if I become a Mormon, it's possible to eventually become a god by an exaltation process, too?"

Ms. Clark said, "Yes."

To this, I asked if the Bible did not say that there is only *one* God.

She said, "Yes, there is only one God . . . over us."

---

3. "The Book of Abraham," in G. A. Smith, *Pearl of Great Price*.
4. McConkie, *Mormon Doctrine*, 428.

Her statement was a basic Mormon idea of God: God is an exalted man and became God from this lesser form; and a plurality of gods exists. All of this implies polytheism. It also implies that if the God *over us* became God, then there was a God before him, and so forth into the eternal past (an *infinite regression* of gods!). We are back to the infinite regression concept again. Ms. Clark admitted that the Mormon Church teaches a system of beings becoming gods and that our God is in the chain of gods.

If this is so, then God is always improving. This implies God is not eternally perfect. Either God is eternally perfect, or he is not. If he *is* eternally perfect, then God cannot be in a system of exaltation. If he is *not*, then he is improving. The Bible never tells us that God improves over time. The Mormon doctrine of God becoming God amidst other gods contradicts our sense of reason and the Bible.

The Mormon Doctrine of God Is Polytheistic

My wife and I were seated in an airport terminal waiting to board a plane when I saw two young men in white shirts, black ties, and black pants walk by, each carrying a briefcase. I nudged my wife and said, "Look, Mormon missionaries. I'll be right back." I walked up to them and saw that each one had a name tag stating he was an elder in the Mormon Church. I introduced myself and asked if I could ask a few questions about their faith.

I probed about what the Mormon concept of God was and how Mormonism started. I received an answer not unlike what Ms. Jones and Ms. Clark gave me. Eventually, I moved the conversation to the idea of multiple gods. I posed the question as to whether this implied polytheism because there was a God over us and gods elsewhere. They said that their doctrine implied polytheism.

I asked, "How then is the Mormon doctrine of plural gods different from Hinduism that asserts the same thing?" Both elders stared at me, and one elder said that they could not answer this question but resorted to the idea that the God over us is the most important. The contradictory implication of a polytheistic universe had not been considered by them before. I shared the biblical concept of God with them.

Mormonism Teaches That the Plurality of Gods Exist

Joseph Smith's great-nephew was Joseph Fielding Smith (J. F. Smith). J. F. Smith compiled a book on the teachings of Joseph Smith.[5] Section 6 therein covers sermons by Joseph Smith in 1843–1844. This section contains a paragraph entitled "Plurality of Gods," in which Joseph Smith says, "I will preach on the plurality of Gods" and then states "there is but one God—that is pertaining to us."[6] The next paragraph is entitled "Scripture Interpretation," in which Joseph Smith claims that "the head of the Gods brought forth the Gods" and that the "head God organized the heavens and the earth," and from a "plurality of Gods . . . . The heads of the Gods appointed one God for us."[7] This is exactly what Ms. Clark's concept was.

The opening pages of J. F. Smith's book state that what is compiled by J. F. Smith are "taken from his [the Prophet Joseph Smith] sermons . . . in the days of the Prophet's ministry."[8] That is, these are purportedly inspired words because they came directly from Joseph Smith.

The Mormon Church founder, Joseph Smith, says this: "God himself was once as we are now, and is an exalted man," and we "have got to learn how to be Gods . . . the same as all Gods have done before" us, "namely, by going . . . from exaltation to exaltation."[9]

In *Mormon Doctrine*, McConkie quotes Joseph Smith as saying, "God himself was once as we are now, and is an exalted man," and "I am going to tell you how God came to be God. We have imagined and supposed that God was God from all eternity. I will refute that idea . . . he was once a man like us."[10]

In Mormon doctrine, God became God via an exaltation process, so God's nature is changeable. This concept is in contradiction to the Bible. Either the God of Mormonism or the God of the Bible is true. To say that they are both true violates the rule of noncontradiction.

---

5. J. Smith, *Teachings of the Prophet*.
6. J. Smith, *Teachings of the Prophet*, 370.
7. J. Smith, *Teachings of the Prophet*, 371–72.
8. J. Smith, *Teachings of the Prophet*, opening unnumbered pages preceding the "Introduction."
9. J. Smith, *Teachings of the Prophet*, 345–47.
10. McConkie, *Mormon Doctrine*, 321.

Sorting through Worldviews

A Discussion on the Head God

The following story shows that if we follow the implications of Mormon concepts of God, the concept leads to unbiblical ideas.

While I was standing in my driveway doing some woodwork one afternoon, two young Mormon male missionaries approached me and asked if I could talk with them. After listening to their opening comments, I asked them about God's nature. Eventually we arrived at multiple gods and that the God over us became God.

In order to reason out the implications of this, I asked some questions. If God became God over us, and other galaxies have a god that became god over them, wouldn't this imply that at some point in the history of the universe, if we reversed the process, wouldn't there be a *Head God* somewhere? I mean, who started this whole process? Whoever started the process would be the Head God, right?

Both missionaries looked at each other, then back at me, and one said, "Who knows? Maybe there is a Head God."

This is an interesting admission, so I pursued it. I said that I was curious about this concept because, if it is true that there was a god before our God, and a god before him, leading backwards to an infinite regression of gods, how could there be a first or Head God? Logically, there would be no beginning to start the series of gods becoming gods. An infinite series is beginning-less, so there is no beginning to move forward from, so how could a progression of men becoming gods be true? Doesn't this exaltation of men to godhood, leading to other gods, a contradictory notion?

I then addressed the Bible, which does not say anything about a Head God leading to a succession of gods sometime in the past or the exaltation of gods from men.

Both missionaries told me that they had never thought about this idea of seeing the origin of God as it relates to the nature of God. This is what we need to pursue as Christians when talking with Mormons. They wished me a good day and told me that they had to go to other appointments.

When we propose these kinds of questions to Mormons, the usual response is that God is an incomprehensible mystery. We can agree but reply that what may be incomprehensible should not be self-contradictory. Because the Bible gives is truth about the nature of God, and because the Bible says that God has always been God, Mormon doctrine must be in error. Mormonism has a theory of God, but such a God could not exist in reality.

The Jesus of Mormonism Reduces Him to Be a Mere Human

Bruce McConkie writes: "Christ was begotten by an Immortal Father in the same way that mortal men are begotten by mortal fathers."[11] This implies that Jesus is in a process of exaltation, which results in the conclusion that the work of Jesus on the cross is insufficient for salvation, because Jesus would be only in the process of perfection. The Mormon concept of Jesus contradicts the opening of the Gospel of John, which states the Word (the Son—Jesus) has been "with God" and "was God" from eternity.

The Rule of Noncontradiction, Mormonism, and the Bible

McConkie states that a "plurality of gods exists," meaning that the Father, Son, and Holy Spirit are "three . . . Gods." He states that along with this Trinity, there is "in addition . . . an infinite number of holy personages drawn from worlds without number, who have passed on to exaltation and are thus gods." He also states that Joseph Smith taught that the Father also has a Father and that this Father "had a Father also."[12] This concept implies an infinite regression of fathers. But if Jesus had a father who also had a father, then Jesus is a *grandson*, which is totally anti-biblical.

Let's apply the biblical revelation of God and logical reasoning to see if Mormonism is contradictory to the Bible by looking at various texts.

Consider Isaiah 43:10, which says, "Before me no god was formed, nor will there be one after me." Mormonism states that prior to God the Father becoming the God over us in our area of the cosmos, there was a god/father before him and so on, back through eternity. However, this text states that "before me," no god existed, which includes our area of the cosmos. This text contradicts Mormonism.

Let's consider statements in Isaiah and Revelation to see if it logically follows that the God over us came to be this God over us. Note that these texts state what God is saying of himself. "I [God] am the first and I am the last" (Isa 44:6 and 48:12). Revelation 21:6 states, "I [God] am . . . the Beginning and the End" (a rephrasing of first and last). We try to reason with Mormons by asking questions. How could the God over us, who followed from an infinite line of succession of prior gods, also be the *first* or

---

11. McConkie, *Mormon Doctrine*, 547.
12. McConkie, *Mormon Doctrine*, 576–77.

the *beginning*? Doesn't reason tell us that there cannot be more than one personal entity that is the first or the beginning? Two beings cannot both be first.

The Bible's concept of God as the only eternal God, and the Mormon concept of God who is in an eternal exaltation process, cannot both be true, because they are mutually exclusive concepts. The rule of noncontradiction eliminates the possibility that both are true. Therefore, only the nature of God as revealed in the Bible can be true.

A Discussion about Jacket Color

Two Mormon elders and I were talking at my front door. They forged ahead with the Mormon doctrine that "God became a God over us from a prior god." I diverted the conversation to one elder, who was wearing a black jacket, by saying, "Your jacket is black. Now suppose I said that it is *true* that your jacket was *completely black*, but your elder friend here said that it was *completely red*." I explained that if I say it's true that it is thoroughly black, it cannot be true that it's simultaneously thoroughly red, because the statements contradict, and what makes a contradiction is that one statement is false.

I asked, "Do you agree that a contradictory argument must be a false argument?"

They both agreed.

I read Isaiah 43:10 from their KJV Bible. It says that there was no God before God and no God after him. I explained that the Mormon doctrine claims that the God over us came from a line of previous gods, but the Bible says the opposite. Therefore, they can't both be correct because they contradict.

I asked, "Which is correct, Mormon doctrine or the Bible?"

They said that all of this was a *mystery*. They did not provide an answer except to say that I was misinterpreting the Bible. In other words, the Bible is interpreted correctly only if it corresponds to Mormon doctrine. I ended the conversation by explaining that the Bible's statements about God and the Mormon statements about God cannot both be true, just like it cannot be true that the jacket was both black and red simultaneously. They needed to decide whether to believe the Bible or Mormon doctrine.

It Is Anti-Bible to Suppose That God Has a Material Body

In a Mormon book of doctrines by one of the Twelve Apostles of the Mormon Church, it is asserted that God the Father possesses "bodily parts."[13] This is contradictory to the Bible, as the following argument by Aquinas shows:[14]

A body is an object that has a perimeter in *space*. For God to have a body contradicts 1 Kings 8:27, which states, "Even the highest heaven cannot contain" God.

A bodily God implies a beginning in *time*. This is contradictory to 2 Timothy 1:9 and Titus 1:2, which state God had interaction with the Son "before the beginning of time." Also, 1 Corinthians 2:7 states that God had wisdom "before time began."

A body is composed of *parts*. For God to be composed of parts, he would have to have been created or have created himself. This contradicts Psalm 90:2, which says God is from "everlasting," and Psalm 93:2, which says God is "from all eternity."

Mormonism's Reliance on a Subjective "Burning in the Bosom"

After an hour-long conversation with two elders in my home, one elder suggested the following: "Pray and ask God if *The Book of Mormon* and the message of the Mormon Church are true." He said that God will make truth known to me through a "burning in the bosom."

I knew of this concept from a verse in *The Book of Mormon*.[15] This idea is also in *Doctrine and Covenants*, section 9, verse 8, wherein God purports to speak to a man named Oliver Cowdery about Joseph Smith's precepts. It says that God "will cause that your [Cowdery's] bosom shall burn within you; therefore, you shall feel that it is right."[16] Mormons claim this feeling as a major sign from God that Mormonism is the true religion.

Mormon missionaries will always ask you to read *The Book of Mormon* and to pray about the truth of their theology. This may be designed

---

13. Talmage, *Articles of Faith*, 41.
14. This is a summary of Aquinas, *Summa Theologica*, part 1, question 3, article 2.
15. Moroni 10:4.
16. G. A. Smith, *Doctrine and Covenants*, 13.

Sorting through Worldviews

to get you to constantly think on the claims of Mormonism until you get a good feeling about their faith and not ask probing questions.

Note two things. First, you are asked to pray about the validity of *The Book of Mormon*, not of the Bible or Jesus Christ. But Jesus says, "He [the Holy Spirit] will testify about me [Jesus]," not some other book (John 15:26). Second, the criteria for determining the validity of Mormonism is a "burning" that is "within" you that makes you "feel" Mormonism is true. It is an appeal to subjectivity. It is an appeal to sense experience over critical thinking and biblical revelation. It's like saying a jacket is thoroughly red because you love the feeling of red, even if it is true that the jacket is thoroughly black.

In an attempt to show the two elders that the Bible is superior to subjective feelings, I gave them an analogy. "I'm married," I said, "but suppose I prayed about instigating an adulterous affair with a lady and felt a strong burning in my bosom to do this. Is this okay to pray about?"

"No, because we already know adultery is wrong."

"And we know this because the Bible tells us so, right?" I asked.

"Yes."

We agreed that the Bible has precedence over a feeling, if the feeling contradicts the Bible. Prayer does not make the feeling correct. I then proposed to the missionaries the principle that if any doctrine of Mormonism is contradictory to the Bible, the doctrine is wrong, regardless of subjective feelings. They responded with the argument that "God gives progressive revelation, so we can believe a later concept, even if it's contradictory to a prior statement in the Bible."[17]

"If so, how can you trust God for truth today, when, tomorrow, God will tell you that it is no longer true?" I asked.

If God can contradict what he says about himself, we might as well argue that even though the Bible says God is spirit, we might discover later that he is really a jolly obese man with a white beard.

The missionaries just looked at each other and, with a proper farewell, left to visit other people.

It is difficult to have a logical discussion on objective truth when someone relies on subjectivism for truth.

---

17. See "Clarity of Terms and Publications" regarding *progressive revelation* at the beginning of this chapter.

God as Mystery

God's realm is a mystery to finite humans. We cannot, however, dismiss contradictory concepts by tossing them into the realm of mystery. Just because some aspects of faith are mysterious is not justification for ignoring the process of thinking through ideas. It is true that we don't know the answer to all mathematical problems, but this does not mean that we can believe that five plus seven equals ninety.

Mormons may resort to Deuteronomy 29:29 to ignore contradictions. This verse states that God has "secrets," which he does not reveal to humans. This is true, but Mormons have misunderstood what verse 29 is talking about. For context, the previous twenty-eight verses speak of God's covenant relationship and his dealings with Israel during their wilderness wandering, which Israel did not completely understand, as verse 4 says (Israel did not have "a mind that understands"). The secrets that God knows in verse 29 are additional information Israel did not know. Verse 29 is not saying that, in God's realm, God's secret is that contradictions make sense. God does not dwell in a reality in which nonsense makes sense. If Mormons assert that, in God's realm, anything is possible, we might as well make the statement that, in God's mysterious realm, triangles could have four sides or that one of God's secrets is that circles have corners.

There Is No Such Thing as a New Version of Christianity

A Mormon friend told me that, in 1830, Joseph Smith was restoring the lost, distorted, and corrupted original message of NT Christianity. If this Mormon message is true, then why can't we find Mormon doctrines in the NT about a series of gods leading to a God over us, or multiple gods elsewhere in the cosmos, or that god is in a body somewhere? We have to wonder how the writers of the twenty-seven books of the NT missed all of this information.

Here is an important principle to keep in mind: an infallible God would not give contradictory and logically inconceivable revelations of himself as time passes.

Book Recommendation

Here is a short list of books presenting biblical Christian, Evangelical views, in contrast to Mormonism:

For a concise comparison between the Bible and Mormon ideas, read Bill McKeever and Eric Johnson's *Mormonism 101*.

For contrasting views on the nature of God discussed by a Mormon scholar, Stephen Robinson, and a biblical scholar, Craig Blomberg, read *How Wide the Divide*.

For an account of public dialogues between a Mormon scholar, Dr. Robert Millet, and a Baptist pastor, Rev. Gregory Johnson, read *Bridging the Divide*.

For a defense of public forums to discuss differences and similarities between Mormonism and Evangelical theology, read *Talking with Mormons*, by the former president of Fuller Theological Seminary, Richard Mouw.

Note: in *How Wide the Divide*, Robinson explains that not all statements made by Mormons on the nature of God reflect "official" Mormon doctrine.[18] In other words, some of the quotes I mentioned in this chapter may not be official doctrine of the Mormon Church. But Mormons do not disagree with these concepts of God either. Robinson says, for example, "Nothing I say . . . should be interpreted as denying" that God has a "nature as an exalted man."[19] And in *Bridging the Divide*, Millet says that Mormons believe that "God is an Exalted Man," as stated by Joseph Smith, and "he is not of a different species with mortal men," and "for us [Mormons] God is a man, a person, an actual being with a glorified and exalted personality."[20]

---

18. Robinson, in Robinson and Blomberg, *How Wide the Divide*, 140.
19. Robinson, in Robinson and Blomberg, *How Wide the Divide*, 91.
20. Millet, in Millet and Johnson, *Bridging the Divide*, 58.

12

Islam

Basic Beliefs, the Quran, and Calmly Conversing with Muslims

Three Main Issues for Discussion

MUSLIMS DENY THE TRINITY, so theological issues are more in line with talking about the Trinity, as outlined in chapter 9. Most Christians are not going to have complicated discussions on the nature of God with a Muslim. Therefore, I offer only some basic insights on various topics that may arise in a discussion. Some are: (1) the Islamic concept of Allah in contrast to God in the New Testament (NT); (2) the Islamic anti-Trinitarian idea in contrast to the Christian doctrine of the Trinity; and (3) the basis for the forgiveness of sins.

Summary Background of Islam

In order for readers to receive the most from this chapter about talking with Muslims, I will give a brief overview of Islam. Further information on Islamic traditions is in the *Encyclopedia of Islam* and *The Oxford Dictionary of Islam*.[1]

---

1. Campo and Melton, *Encylopedia of Islam;* Esposito, *Oxford Dictionary of Islam*.

Sorting through Worldviews

Islam, Judaism, and Christianity's Common Ancestry

These three religions are tied to Abraham of the Hebrew Scriptures that are sometimes called the Old Testament by Christians. They diverge from Abraham's two sons: Ishmael, the firstborn, and Isaac, the second born. Islam is derived from the lineage of Ishmael. Judaism and Christianity are derived from the lineage of Isaac, including Isaac's son, Jacob. Jacob, whose name was changed to Israel, had twelve sons, later called the twelve tribes of Israel. Jesus came from one of the twelve tribes, Judah.

Muhammad

Muhammad was born about AD 570, in Mecca, in current Saudi Arabia. Both parents died by the time he was six years old. His grandfather raised him for two years, and then his grandfather died. Muhammad's uncle, Abu Talib, raised Muhammad until Muhammad became an adult. Muhammad claims that when he was about forty years old, about AD 610, he was in a cave, when the angel Gabriel appeared and began to give him the words that would gradually become the Quran (surah 25:32).[2]

Islam/Muslim Defined

The term Islam means submission or surrender to Allah. A Muslim is "one who surrenders" and "one who accepts Muhammad as God's prophet and the Quran as God's word."[3]

Two major traditions of Islam are *Sunni* and *Shia*. They are the result of the controversy as to who was the legitimate successor of Muhammad.

A *Sunni* claims that no successor was named, so Muhammad's father-in-law, Abu Bakr, succeeded him. Sunni Muslims make up about 85 percent of all Muslims and tend towards a stricter expression of Islam than Shiites.

A *Shiite* claims that Muhammad elected his cousin and son-in-law, Ali Talib, to succeed him. Ali was married to Muhammad's daughter.

---

2. Quran references are from the Quran translation by Muslim scholar Ali. Sometimes Quran is spelled as Koran. The Quran consists of surahs (pronounced like *soo-rah*). These act as chapters. For example, surah 25 means chapter 25.

3. Lawrence, "Muslim."

Shiites claim a family connection to Muhammad. Shiite is from *Shiat-Ali*, or "party of Ali."

Five Characteristics of Islam

Anees Zaka is the founder of the Biblical Institute for Islamic Studies in Philadelphia. In an essay, she says that "Islam is a religion that applies differently to different categories of people in any Muslim society," but "Islam may be summarized" in five "essential assumptions." My restated version of her five areas is summarized as follows.

1. Humans are not created in God's image and are not sinners with a fallen nature, so we do not need a Savior like Jesus.
2. Human effort to conform to Allah's will determine one's destiny; therefore, eternal life is not assured.
3. Muhammad is the ultimate prophet.
4. Islam is a belief system and "a re-statement of what Allah has said to man."
5. Islam is expressed in the form of laws that dictate what is right in life.[4]

Central Message of Islam

Religious scholars Juan Campo and J. Gordon Melton state that the basic Islamic belief is this: "There is no god but God, and Muhammad is his messenger."[5] Attesting to this statement constitutes an "affirmation of membership in the Community . . . of Muslims."[6] Campo and Melton list five pillars of Islamic beliefs, and this statement is the first one. The other four pillars are prayer, almsgiving, fasting, and a pilgrimage to Mecca once in a lifetime.[7]

---

4. Zaka, "Here I Stand," 61–62.
5. Campo and Melton, *Encyclopedia of Islam*, 373.
6. Campo and Melton, *Encyclopedia of Islam*, 618.
7. Campo and Melton, *Encyclopedia of Islam*, 242–43.

Douglas Pratt writes that Islam has a "range of theological . . . positions," and a dialogue between us can honor the moral values of Muslims while seeking peaceful interaction over theological differences.[8]

The rest of this chapter highlights only the *theological differences* between Islam and Christianity, so that Christians can peacefully discuss the nature of God and Christ with Muslims.

Islam's Quran Contrasted with the Christian Scriptures

Quran means recitation, and it is the Islamic Holy Book originally written in Arabic. The Quran was dictated to scribes by one person, Muhammad, over a period of twenty-three years (about AD 610–633). It consists of 114 sections/chapters called a *surah*. Each surah (chapter) contains verses. A strict Muslim would hold that the Quran must be read in Arabic if one wants to read it as the word of God, because there is really only one Quran.

In contrast, the Bible is composed of multiple authors writing over 1,500 years and contains sixty-six sections called books. The Hebrew Scriptures (OT) were originally written in Hebrew, with some portions in Aramaic. The NT books were written in Koine Greek. Current NT translations are compiled from thousands of Greek texts from the second century onward and can be put into many languages, yet still retain their value as the word of God.

The overarching messages of the Quran and the Bible are not the same. First, we must define the term *God*; otherwise, we might think that we're talking to a Muslim with the same concept of God as in the Bible.

Allah in the Quran Is Not the Biblical God

The Arabic word for God is *Allah*. Christians can speak with Muslims about God using the word Allah in the same sense that Christians can use the Hebrew word Yahweh when talking to Jews about God. But there is a difference between Islamic and Christian concepts of God, which we will see in the following paragraphs.

The Quran gives ninety-nine names—attributes—of Allah. (Some of Allah's names are in surah 59:22–24.) The Islamic list of names with brief

---

8. Pratt, "Religious Pluralism and Dialogue," 113, 123.

corresponding definitions is in *Answering Islam* by Norman Geisler and Abdul Saleeb.[9]

Muslims and Christians agree on some general concepts of God: Allah is the creator of the universe, so pantheism is denied, just as pantheism is denied in Christianity. Allah is eternal, perfectly moral, and sovereign over the universe, just as God is in Christianity.

Islam and Christianity agree that there is only one God (monotheism) but differ on the definition of one. Allah, in Islam, does not have a plural nature, so *one* means that Allah is a singular spiritual Being. Muslims deny the Christian doctrine of the Trinity, stating that it implies three gods, so Christianity is therefore polytheistic. Surah 4:171 says to "desist" from saying "Trinity," because "Allah is One God." Surah 5:73 states that to say "Allah is one of three in a Trinity" is to "blaspheme" (to speak evil).

Christianity claims *Trinitarian monotheism*: there is *one* God who is three in persons. This is unlike Allah in Islam. Islam and Christianity contradict each other about God's nature, so they cannot both be correct. Therefore, when Christians talk with Muslims about God, or Allah, we are not talking about the same God, even though we use the same term.

Islam Mistakenly Claims That Christianity is Polytheistic

"You Christians believe in three gods, and this is polytheistic," a Muslim man said.

I asked a nonconfrontational question: "Interesting, but how did you come to this conclusion?"

"The Father is god, the Son is god, and the Spirit is god—therefore, three gods."

"I think you might have a misconception of what Trinity means because you see it as a math problem," I said.

"Give me your explanation."

I explained that the Trinity is one God expressed as an internal relationship in three persons, but not three separate gods as in polytheism. The Trinity is understood as a moral revelation of God, not a math problem to solve. If Allah is a lone entity, why would Allah have a desire to create a universe with moral human beings, since Allah had no experience as relating to persons in his nature? Muslims live in loving relationships created

---

9. Geisler and Saleeb, *Answering Islam*, 23–27.

by Allah but deny that Allah is an eternal relationship in his nature. This is inconsistent.

Kenneth Bailey says that in the Quran we "can read about 'God,' the 'Word of God,' and the 'Spirit of God,'" as in the doctrine of the Trinity, but Islam does not "reflect on how those three Quranic descriptions of the divine come together."[10] In our discussion with Muslims, we can show that there is a point of contact with them in theology and help bring the descriptions of God together into the biblical Trinity understanding.

Jesus in the Quran Is Not the Jesus of the NT

Jesus (*Isa* in Arabic) is mentioned in the Quran. The following surah references from the Quran show various concepts of Jesus compared to the NT.

Quranic statements consistent with the Bible:

- Jesus was the "son of Mary," a virgin (3:45–47).
- Jesus is called "Christ," the term for Messiah (3:45).
- Jesus performed healing miracles to "those born blind, and the lepers, and . . . quicken[ed] the dead" (3:49).

Quranic statements contradicting the Bible:

- "The similitude of Jesus . . . is as that of Adam; [Allah] created him from dust" (3:29). This is the opposite of John 1:1, which states that Jesus had no beginning.
- It is "monstrous" to claim that Allah "has begotten a son" (19:88–89). Allah "begetteth not" (112:3). John 3:16, in the King James Version, contradicts this. The term "begotten" used in the KJV is replaced with "one and only Son" in most other English Bibles.
- Allah's "curse" is on "Christians [who] call Christ the son of God" (9:30). This contradicts 1 John 4:15, which says, "If anyone acknowledges that Jesus is the Son of God, God lives in them."
- Jesus was a "Messenger of Allah" (4:157), and "no more than a Messenger," and one of "many" other messengers (5:73). This contradicts John 14:6, where Jesus says, "I am the way and the truth and the life. No one comes to the Father except through me."

---

10. Bailey, *Paul through Mediterranean Eyes*, 115.

- Jesus's was "made to appear" as dying on the cross (4:157). This contradicts 1 Corinthians 15:3, which states Christ actually died.

Islam and Christianity contradict each other about Jesus, so they cannot both be correct. Therefore, when Christians talk with Muslims about Jesus, we are not talking about the same Jesus.

Sin, Future Judgment, and Salvation in Islam

"Islam does not believe that humanity is sinful."[11] In Islamic theology, "sin is not original," and "man [humankind] . . . is not a fallen being."[12] Muslim scholar Tariq Ramadan says that "the notion of original sin does not exist in Islam: humanity is born innocent."[13] Muslims do not deny that they have sinned (surah 9:66), but we do not need a Savior like Jesus. There is no mention in the Quran of a personal sacrifice to pay for the moral debt of sin, as opposed to the NT revelation that Jesus died for the sins of the world.

Future *judgment* for the Muslim is based on individual performance. Surah 9 gives the Islamic view of repentance, which includes turning from bad deeds, just like Christianity, but does not include seeking forgiveness in a personal Savior. Surah 66:8 says, "Turn to Allah with sincere repentance: in the hope that your Lord will remove from you your ills and admit you to Gardens [of Paradise]." Note that salvation is only a hope, instead of a surety. In Islam, there is no way a person can be assured of salvation, because it is impossible to know how good you have to be to qualify for salvation. In regards to judgment in Christianity, Jesus is the one who judges us, and this is the same Jesus who died for us.

For a Muslim, *salvation* is the result of human works. For example: "To those who believe and do deeds of righteousness hath Allah promised forgiveness" (5:9). And, "on those who believe and work deeds of righteousness, will (Allah) Most Gracious bestow love" (19:96). Allah "listens to those who believe and do deeds of righteousness" (42:26). Basically, Allah looks to see how the balance of good and bad deeds compares: "Then those whose balance (of good deeds) is heavy—they will attain salvation," but if the "balance" of good deeds is "light," then these will "have lost their souls" (23:102–3).

11. Kateregga and Shenk, *Muslim and Christian*, 45.
12. Kateregga and Shenk, *Muslim and Christian*, 141.
13. Ramadan, "Muslims, Prophethood, and Jesus," 49.

No one knows if his or her scale is balanced towards good deeds. How can I increase the weight on the good side of the scale, or how can I pay for my moral debt of sin, when I am the actual problem? It's like paying my bills with counterfeit money. There is no concept in Islam that moral debt is paid by anyone. This is why Islam offers only a "hope" for the future.

In Christ, God is not a moral accountant, because it was Jesus who paid our debt. Salvation is either by God's free grace or not. If not, then it's by works. In contradiction to Islam, the Bible tells us that salvation is "by grace . . . not by works" (Eph 2:8–9).

Center for Islamic Research and Awareness International

CIRA is a Christian-based ministry designed to contribute to Christian and Muslim dialogue. It was founded by former Muslim Al Fadi, of Saudi Arabia. A testimony by Mr. Fadi, given on January 25, 2019, can be viewed on YouTube.[14]

A Muslim Doctor's Story

Several years ago, I was introduced to a medical doctor and a Christian convert from Islam, Dr. Ahmed Joktan. The doctor was visiting America from his home in Saudi Arabia at that time. He spent several hours telling me his story, which was published in 2020 in a book entitled *From Mecca to Christ*.

Dr. Joktan wrote that he is the son of a Saudi Islamic scholar called a *mufti*. During medical school studies, Joktan had a dream of Jesus that led him on a journey to become a Christian. His family discovered a Bible in his bedroom, which gave them evidence of his connection to Christianity. As a result, several of his Muslim brothers beat him and then secured him in a tent outside of the family house. His father later entered the tent with an assault rifle, demanding that he renounce Christianity. His book outlines his Christian journey and a perspective of what life is like for believers in Jesus who live in Saudi Arabia.

---

14. https://www.youtube.com/watch?v=6ialwVGFAmA. See https://cirainternational.com for additional information on Islam from Al Fadi.

Islam

Discussions with Muslims

The late Rick Love was known worldwide as an expert in forging Christian and Muslim relations. He was the president of Peace Catalyst International.[15] In his book *Peace Catalysts*, he outlines how important it is to be a peacemaker. This is a very important book for our times.

Love advises us that "the Muslim world is radically diverse," with over "1.5 billion Muslims" and "huge variations in expressions of Islam."[16] Therefore, as we get to know our Muslim neighbors, we are free to ask about where they are from, their specific Islamic background, and how they see Islam practiced. This will lead to an engaging dialogue, creating a bridge to Christianity.

Book Recommendation

To obtain a basic understanding of the Quran by a former Muslim, now a biblical scholar, see *Understanding the Koran* by Mateen Elass. For a comprehensive study of Islam see *Islam* by Hans Küng.

---

15. See www.peacecatalyst.org.
16. Love, *Peace Catalysts*, 89.

13

Conversing with the Jewish Traditions
The Three Jewish Worldviews and Jesus as Messiah

Jewish Tradition

I RECEIVED A SUBSTANTIAL education in Judaism after attending a Sabbath meeting in a synagogue. I learned that there are three overarching views of Judaism after I asked the rabbi a question.

"Since the Hebrew Scriptures speak of animal sacrifices by appointed priests in a temple in Jerusalem for the forgiveness of sins, yet there is none of this today, how are your sins forgiven?" I naïvely and arrogantly thought I had him on this and was prepared to give my Christian view that Jesus fulfilled the need for their system.

The rabbi told me that my view was outside of the Jewish traditions and was too literalistic. He said Jewish tradition matters, not a literal view of the Hebrew Scriptures. He said, for example, suppose the synagogue leaders were meeting to discuss a new paint color for the synagogue walls that had been traditionally blue for two hundred years. Then an angel walks in and says that God wants green walls. The rabbi said that the leaders would still paint the walls blue, because that had been their tradition.

My attempt at evangelical entrapment dissolved, and I was rendered speechless. The rabbi told me that his synagogue was within the Reformed Jewish tradition and that there were three main views in Judaism: *Reformed,*

Conservative, and *Orthodox*. I had had no idea that there was a threefold expression of Judaism.

The Reformed view adheres to traditions over a literal reading of the Hebrew Scriptures. The Orthodox rests on a more literal and historical reading of Scripture. The Conservative view is somewhere in between. It is necessary to discern what worldview a Jewish person has when trying to talk to them about Christ and the Bible.[1] Bible scholar N. T. Wright says that when we speak of first-century Judaism, it is "best to speak of Judaisms" in the "plural," because "Jews do not characteristically describe . . . Judaism in terms of beliefs."[2]

Defining Messiah

This term *messiah* is a Hebrew term meaning "to anoint." In 1 Samuel 16:13, for example, David has oil poured over him to "anoint him" as Israel's king, which act was a way to designate and appoint him "with divine authority."[3] The consistently used NT Greek equivalent term for messiah is *Christ*.

First-Century Jewish Idea of a Messiah

Wright says that "there was no single . . . 'messianic expectation' among first-century Jews."[4] Wright highlights a few concepts that first-century Jews would expect from their messiah: messianic expectations were more for national Israel as a means of "liberation" and "reinstatement as the true people of . . . God," which would "involve military action" in some form. A suffering messiah was not in their view.[5]

John Goldingay, an OT scholar, ties the understanding of how Israel thought of a messiah to how Israel thought of a king. Jesus's genealogy ties Jesus to Israel as the "Davidic king."[6] Elsewhere, Goldingay explains that this king-like messiah would come as a "new David . . . who brings [peace]

---

1. The website www.simpletoremember.com broadly outlines these three Jewish views.
2. Wright, *New Testament and People*, 245–46.
3. Waltke, *Old Testament Theology*, 887–88.
4. Waltke, *Old Testament Theology*, 307.
5. Wright, *New Testament and People*, 320.
6. Goldingay, *Israel's Gospel*, 815.

to Israel.[7] Jewish scholar and Christian convert Alfred Edersheim (d. 1889) says that the ancient Jewish concept of a messiah would be one who was "above the ordinary human," but there would still be a "boundary-line separating [messiah] from Divine Personality."[8]

In other words, the kind of messiah that first-century Jews expected was a divinely appointed man—not a divine man—who would lead Israel out of physical Roman dominion, thereby making Israel the number one nation. A messiah would do this in a "political or military" way.[9]

This is not the story of Jesus. The NT portrays Jesus as the Messiah, but not as first-century Jews had expected. If Jesus had been inventing himself as the Messiah, why was he so unlike the expectations?

No One Would Have Invented an Unlikely Messiah like Jesus

Suppose Jesus wanted to falsely pass himself off as an anticipated messiah. It seems that he would have said things and acted like what was *expected* of a Jewish messiah. He would have played the part. But he did not. Furthermore, if the first-century Jewish disciples of Jesus were to pass off Jesus as a messiah, knowing he was not, they would not have invented the most unlikely of messiahs. The record we have of Jesus in the four Gospels shows elements of Jesus that were contrary to the prevailing worldviews of Jews, Greeks, and Romans.

If the Gospel stories of Jesus were invented, then it is unlikely that first-century Jewish writers in Israel would have presented this Messiah with the following characteristics.

- Have the Messiah as a baby laid in a cattle trough called a manger (Luke 2:12)
- Have the Messiah come through a woman without a man involved—the "virgin birth" (Matt 1:18; Luke 1:26–34)
- Have the Messiah's genealogy sprinkled with Gentile women (Rahab and Ruth, listed in Matt 1:5)
- Have the Messiah raised in a town, Nazareth, that had a reputation of nothing good coming from there (John 1:46)

---

7. Goldingay, *Israel's Faith*, 476.
8. Edersheim, *Life and Times*, 1:171.
9. D. Harris, "Messianic Expectations," 758.

- Have the Messiah alone with women and talking to them (John 4)
- Have the Messiah touching people with diseases (a leper in Luke 5:13) or eating with them (Mark 14:3)
- Have the Messiah breaking Jewish laws, which angered the Jewish leaders (Mark 2:24)
- Have the Messiah claiming superiority as the Lord over the holiest day of the week for Jews—the Sabbath day (Mark 2:27)
- Have the Messiah making claims of divinity, when all Jews thought this claim was blasphemous and worthy of death (John 5:18; 10:33)
- Have the Messiah beaten and then crucified by Israel's pagan enemies, the Romans (Matt 27:27–31)
- Have the Messiah, on resurrection morning, appear first to women, and then have the women tell the men of his resurrection (Matt 28:1, 10)

Conversation with a Reformed Jewish Man

On an airplane flight, I sat next to a man, and we discussed the books we were reading. He told me that he was Jewish. After some preliminaries, I asked him how he saw a messiah coming from Abraham, as told in Jewish Scriptures. He said that Abraham was not a historical person and only represented the Jewish people as a symbol of them. This man said that he was ethnically and traditionally Jewish in the Reformed tradition but knew nothing of the Hebrew Bible.

To stall for thinking time, I said, "Interesting that you said this." Then I mentioned that the Jesus of the Bible was ethnically and traditionally Jewish as well, but Jesus claimed that he was Israel's Messiah. I asked him what he thought of this claim.

He said, "I do not think of it, because it means nothing to me."

I said, "Well, let me get your opinion on an idea. Don't you think it odd that Jesus would claim to be Israel's awaited Messiah, yet be opposite from what Israel expected in a messiah?"

He asked me what I meant by this.

I offered a few examples. Jesus was born and raised in Israel and knew Jewish traditions and Scriptures. But then as an adult, he violated Jewish customs, walked around criticizing the Jewish religious leaders, and, to get even weirder, he was killed by Israel's enemies at the time, the Romans.

Sorting through Worldviews

What true messiah would do that? He did think it odd but said that this was Jesus's consequences for claiming that he was the Jewish Messiah. I suggested that he should consider checking out the book of Genesis, because it is the story of how Israel originated, and the NT rests on a real historical Abraham. The conversation moved to other topics.

Reformed vs. Orthodox Judaism

Over a period of eighteen months, Reformed Rabbi Ammiel Hirsch and Orthodox Rabbi Yosef Reinman exchanged emails debating the differences in their faith traditions, and then the emails were put into a book. Reiman's view is that the *Torah* (the first five books of the Bible, Genesis through Deuteronomy) is reliable as an historical witness of God. He points out that the books of Exodus through Deuteronomy document the forty years Israel spent wandering the desert wherein miracles were seen, but if this record is false, "no one would have accepted" the Torah as divine revelation.[10] Hirsch says, "I do not accept the Torah as the literal word of God."[11] For Hirsch, Judaism is "by . . . membership in the Jewish people"[12] and tied to the ethnicity of being Jewish and to those traditions.

It is important to know what the Jewish person's worldview tradition is as we attempt a dialogue about Christ. Asking questions without judgment is the only way to begin.

New Testament Examples

The following two examples from Luke show stories that are too un-Jewish and un-messiah-like in character to have been invented by first-century Christians who expected Jews to believe that Jesus is the true Messiah, unless the stories were true.

Jesus tells a parable of a Samaritan helping a robbery victim after several Jewish religious leaders from Jerusalem passed by without helping (Luke 10:25–37). The hero of the story is a Samaritan! Jewish religious leaders in Jerusalem looked down upon Samaritans in the first century.[13] The

---

10. Hirsch and Reinman, *One People, Two Worlds*, 125.
11. Hirsch and Reinman, *One People, Two Worlds*, 37.
12. Hirsch and Reinman, *One People, Two Worlds*, 267.
13. Samaria is a region north of Jerusalem. In 722 BC, Assyria conquered this region. Eventually, Samaritan Jews became more Greek-like, while Jerusalem Jews retained

story was highly insulting to the Jewish religious leaders whom Luke was intending to convert to Christianity. Luke would not have included a story of Jesus claiming to be the Jewish Messiah and then making a Samaritan the hero, unless the story were true.

In Luke 7:36–50, Jesus is in the home of a Pharisee, a lay Jewish religious leader. The story includes a woman. Note two things about this woman that are completely *countercultural*. First, she is called a "sinner" and is in a Pharisee's home. Second, she touches Jesus, a rabbi. Unless this story is true, no first-century writer would have included it in his Gospel account, because it is un-messiah-like.

For further reading on Jesus's life and words in the Middle Eastern culture of the first century, see *Jesus through Middle Eastern Eyes*.[14]

The Salvation of Romans, Too

Israel's religious leaders expected a messiah to save them from Roman oppression. Jesus came and told these leaders that he wanted to save Israel *and* the Romans. No one would invent a messiah and have this fake messiah make these overtures, because that would be too un-messiah-like.

OT Prophecies That Jesus Could Not Have Faked Fulfilling

There are events recorded in the four Gospels that Jesus could not have self-fulfilled in order to trick people into thinking he was the Messiah.

Jesus's body was beaten, scourged (flogged), and pierced by Roman soldiers. Texts in Isaiah 53:4–5 and Zechariah 12:10 speak of this. The NT record states that this happened (Matt 27:26 and John 19:1). Jesus had no control over the details of how the Romans would treat him.

Roman soldiers gambled for Jesus's clothing. This is predicted in Psalm 22:18. John 19:23 shows that it happened. Jesus could not have arranged for a gambling episode.

Roman soldiers did not break Jesus's legs at the crucifixion. It was prophesied in Psalm 34:20 that Jesus's bones would not be broken during crucifixion. John 19:33 states that the Roman soldiers did not break Jesus's

---

traditional Judaism and felt superior to Samaritans. See Walton and Keener, *NIV Cultural Backgrounds*, 1812; Freedman et al., "Samaria" and "Samaritans," in *Eerdmans Dictionary of Bible*, 1155–60.

14. Bailey, *Jesus through Middle Eastern Eyes*, 240.

leg bones. Sometimes a block of wood was attached to the cross beneath the victim's feet so that the victim could push up to breathe better and relieve stress on the arms. But it also prolonged the victim's torture. "To end the torture, a victim's legs could be broken, after which death would quickly follow."[15] Jesus would expect that his bones would be broken; he could not have arranged otherwise.

Events like these could not have been coincidental. Nor could these events have been arranged by Jesus or his disciples. This indicates that the Gospel accounts are authentic and divinely inspired connections to the Hebrew Scriptures, showing Jesus as the true Messiah.

---

15. Walton and Keener, "The Crucifixion," in *NIV Cultural Backgrounds*, 1852.

14

The Eastern Religious Worldview
Karma, Luck, and New Age Mystical Spirituality

Applying Concepts of God

CHAPTERS 14 AND 15 will be a movement into worldviews that have no direct written theological dogma. However, we need to *think theologically* in order to converse with proponents of mystical concepts. This will be a trek through the surreal, but more fun than just comparing biblical texts with other religious texts.

Defining the Eastern Religious Worldview

Christian spirituality includes being able to discern the difference between true biblical thinking and false philosophical concepts, so that we do not adopt an Eastern idea and think it is a biblical one. This chapter will help us identify an Eastern philosophical worldview, so we can sort out the underlying contradictions of it in light of what the Bible teaches about spiritual truth.

Eastern religious philosophy is expressed in various forms of Hinduism, Buddhism, Zen Buddhism, Taoism,[1] and New Age spirituality. Some overlapping concepts of Eastern religions are karma, pantheism, and illusion.

---

1. "Tao" is pronounced "Dow," as in the Dow Jones Industrial Average.

Brahman in Hinduism

In the ancient Hindu texts called the Upanishads, "Brahman... is the Ultimate... the Absolute, Totality, the One beyond which there is nothing" and is seen as "the unity of existence," which "includes... the physical universe, space, everything."[2] This is another way to describe pantheism, which was discussed in chapter 5.

Karma

The word *karma* is sometimes referred to by the phrase *transmigration of the soul* or the word *reincarnation*. Karma is the "consequence... or... the sum of all consequences" of "mental or physical action" or "the chain of cause and effect in the world of morality."[3] The current Dalai Lama of Tibetan Buddhism defines karma as the "laws of causality" whereby the actions of a person as "an agent" produce events in the world, which can bring suffering or some positive outcome or something neutral.[4]

The human being works through the karmic process by "the cycle of birth, death, and rebirth," which is called *samsara*, and this process ends when the person becomes aware of his or her "identity with *brahman*."[5] The goal of karma is *nirvana*, which is "a state of liberation or illumination" resulting in freedom from "rebirth."[6]

The process of karma leading to nirvana is the opposite of going to heaven in Christianity, because heaven is not the end result of reincarnation. Souls go to heaven because of the forgiveness of sin by Jesus's sacrificial death and subsequent resurrection from the dead. Heaven is not the result of human works.

The Luck of Buddhism

There is a restaurant owned by a man that I know quite well. Over the entrance to the kitchen area, he has a small platform on which he places a small Buddha statue next to several bowls and glassware. During lunch one

---

2. Organ, *Hinduism*, 108.
3. Schuhmacher et al., *Encyclopedia of Eastern Philosophy*, 175.
4. Mehrotra, *Essential Dalai Lama*, 85–86.
5. Schuhmacher et al., *Encyclopedia of Eastern Philosophy*, 298.
6. Schuhmacher et al., *Encyclopedia of Eastern Philosophy*, 248–49.

day, I asked him what he placed in the containers and why. He said they contain offerings of various pieces of fruit or vegetables and some form of liquid or water. He said that he was a Buddhist and that it was for "good luck."

"What is an example of good luck?" I asked.

"Finding a ten-dollar bill would be good luck."

"And bad luck for whoever lost it. How does luck work?" I asked.

"We make our own luck, or karma," he answered.

"Who's in charge of luck?"

"I don't understand the question," he said.

"Who decides whether good or bad luck is dispensed?"

He did not know.

I inquired as to whether the concept of receiving good or bad luck implied that there was some sort of mind or intellect that knew the difference between good and bad acts and then gives good or bad luck accordingly. Dispensing good/bad luck, or karma, implies a mind to run the system. My friend said that he had no idea how the program of luck worked. It makes sense that he would not know, because a metaphysical luck group defies reason.

Snails and Karma

During my career as a police officer, I worked a one-day shift with another officer. In one of several conversations, I asked if he had a religious background. He said that he had always been a Buddhist, so naturally I asked about his faith. He said, "Buddhism teaches us to be a good person, treat people well, and we receive good luck in return." I asked if this were something like karma, and he said luck and karma were the same. He affirmed that our eternal soul is reincarnated into a body, possibly millions of times, until the karmic cycle is no longer needed, because we reached the eternal blissful state of nirvana.

I asked, "Does this imply that if I live a good life I would come back as a better person? But if I live a bad life, I could come back as a lesser creature?"

He said that is how karma and the rebirth cycle worked.

"What about snails?" I asked.

"Snails?"

"Yeah . . . what bad stuff would a creature do that causes it to reincarnate as a snail?"

While he thought on this, I posed some follow-up questions. "As a snail, how could it have good or bad karma? Is there some sort of 'snail-ness' that the snail conformed to that would qualify it for a better life next time around? Is there a cosmic karma committee that keeps track of this?"

With a broad grin, he admitted that he knew nothing about snails and karma.

My friend asked what my religious view was. I told him that I was a Christian, and Christianity is based on the person of Jesus, not an impersonal cosmic system of reincarnation. Eternal life results from putting our faith in Christ who forgives us of our sin. Christianity answers the human desire for a future with a personal God. The concept of God as personal was not something he had previously considered but said he would think about it.

Who Is in Charge?

I always ask proponents of karma, or luck, "Who's in charge?" Dispensing good or bad luck requires an objective mind that decides between these two opposites. But in Eastern thought, there is no mind outside of the cosmic system, so no Being can make a decision; good and bad are equal. This is contradictory.

The Karma or Luck Concept Is Impersonal

In Eastern pantheism, the universe itself is a luck-dispensing cosmic consciousness operating on an impersonal reward/punishment system: we get what we deserve. We have no one to ask if we need some kind of healing, because there is no such thing as a luck god. We are not forgiven for bad acts; we just endure bad karma or do good deeds, until we can get balanced out. We cannot pray to karma for grace. This is the opposite of Christianity, in which we can pray to a personal God and find grace and help in time of need (Heb 4:16).

Karma Cannot Be an Infinite Process

A woman I know replied to my inquiry as to how her week had been by saying that it had been good, because "I must have good karma this week."

I said that karma is an interesting concept, and then I asked if she thought karma was a real force in the universe, and she said, "Maybe." I asked if she thought that she is going through numerous lives to work off bad karma and that one day she would enter nirvana. "Possibly," she said.

"Do you think," I continued, "that there was a time when you did not exist but were created, which would give you a beginning in time?"

She thought so, she said.

"Since at one time you did not exist," I said, "how did you acquire bad karma at your beginning?" I presented an idea to her. Entering nirvana is what happens when you have no bad karma. If at one time she did not exist, then there would not have been bad karma to work off when she began to exist; therefore, she would have gone to nirvana immediately and would not be standing with me in the present time. To scurry the conversation along, I said that maybe the opposite was true: she always existed and is in an infinite process of working off bad karma. She conceded: "This may be a better view." But then I asked, "If this is an infinite process [the infinite regression view], wouldn't you have worked off bad karma in the infinite past, in which case you'd be in nirvana already and would not be standing with me in the present time?" She said that she had no opinion on this concept.

I explained to her why I was asking. No matter which view she held, she should be *in nirvana now*, but since she is not, this indicates that the karmic philosophy is fatally flawed. I proposed the Christian idea that we have eternal life in Christ by forgiveness of sins, and this does not imply a contradiction. We have talked again on these topics over the years.

Cycle of Rebirth as Liberation vs. Jesus as Savior from Sin

Eastern religions propose the concept of *samsara*: "The cycle of birth, death, and rebirth, to which every human being is subject so long as we live in ignorance and do not know our identity with" the ultimate reality, known as "brahman."[7] Westerners call this idea reincarnation.

In Hinduism, liberation from samsara/karma is by union with ultimate reality or God. This is called reaching *moksha*, "the final liberation . . . from all worldly bonds."[8]

In Buddhism, liberation from samsara is not uniting with a personal God but "enlightenment" or "awakening," in which one is free from ego

---

7. Schuhmacher et al., *Encyclopedia of Eastern Philosophy*, 298.
8. Schuhmacher et al., *Encyclopedia of Eastern Philosophy*, 229.

desires that produce anxiety. Buddhism is "a religion of enlightenment."[9] A person "begins to think Buddhistically when he becomes aware, physically and mentally, of himself in his natural and social environment."[10]

God is internal—within us—in the various forms of Eastern philosophy. As long as we remain ignorant of the God within us, we continue in the cycle of samsara. Ignorance, not sin, is the human problem. In contrast, the Bible states that God is *external* to everything in the cosmos, because God created it. Jesus came to save us from sin, not ignorance, by his once-for-all sacrifice. We cannot live enough lifetimes to earn it.

Buddhism

Buddhism is a philosophy of life more than a religion. It is based on the teachings of Siddhartha Gautama (born about 560 BC in India) who is known as *The Buddha*. The term *Buddha* means "enlightened or awakened."[11] Enlightenment is the essence of Buddhism. Without enlightenment, there is no Buddhism.[12]

The core of Buddhism is found in the *Four Noble Truths*.[13] They are: (1) suffering exists; (2) desire causes suffering; (3) we stop suffering by stopping desire; and (4) we must follow the *Eightfold Path* to do this. The Eightfold Path consists of a list of eight moral principles to live by—to live rightly. As general moral principles, they are not in conflict with any moral precepts in Christianity.

Note one important detail: Buddhism begins with suffering but does not tie it to a first cause in history as in the biblical Adam. Buddhism denies that our selfish desires are rooted in personal sin that must be forgiven by a divine person. Buddhism offers nothing in regards to forgiveness, as in Christianity, thereby rendering Jesus unnecessary.

---

9. Schuhmacher et al., *Encyclopedia of Eastern Philosophy*, 101.
10. Gard, *Buddhism*, 107.
11. Saddhatissa, *Buddha's Way*, 19.
12. Kyokai, *Teaching of Buddha*, 48.
13. Caner, "Buddhism," 114.

Jesus Was Not a Buddhist

A friend once asked me, "Do you think Jesus went to India to study Buddhism?"

Using the method of answering a question with a question, I responded with two questions: "Do you think this happened?" He said that it seemed true. My second question: "Can I ask how you came to this conclusion?" He said that Buddha's moral teaching of the Eightfold Path and Jesus's teachings were alike, and since Buddhism came four hundred years before Jesus, Jesus learned moral principles in India.

Instead of pelting him with biblical quotes, I proposed an analogy. Suppose there were ten "living" houses (houses with a soul) built one after the other, and each house was similar to the previous house. Is it logical to conclude that the first living house contributed to the character of the second house, and eventually the tenth house came from the previous ninth house? Or is it more likely that the similarity of the tenth house to the previous nine is due to a *common builder*? Since God is the Creator of all humans as the common builder, it is reasonable to think that God implanted within all humans the moral notions we have. Therefore, it makes sense that Buddha and Jesus would have common moral values. I added that there are no references in the four Gospels to any Eastern religious philosophy. All references in the Gospels to moral or theological concepts that existed before Jesus come from the Hebrew Scriptures, not to writings in Eastern thought.

His theory actually shows that all humans were created in God's personal moral image more than it shows that Jesus studied Buddhism. He agreed and abandoned his Jesus-was-a-Buddhist theory.

Hindu Pantheism and New Age Spirituality

The Hindu and New Age pantheistic concepts can be summarized as: *Atman is Brahman*. That is, Atman (the Self) is Brahman (Ultimate Reality). The individual soul is really "the ultimate essence of the universe . . . . Atman equals Brahman, Brahman equals Atman."[14] A pantheist is "one who holds both that everything there is constitutes a unity and that this unity is divine . . . . Pantheists thus deny the radical distinction between God

---

14. Ashby, "Hinduism," 309.

and creatures."[15] In other words, in biblical Christianity, there is an infinite quality distinction between divinity and humanity. But, as Hindu and the New Age teach, if each Atman (all humans) are Brahman (divinity), without distinction, then how can there be an Atman who is an atheist? Wouldn't this be God denying himself? We should ask: how would Brahman *not* know he was each Atman?

Maybe All Is an Illusion

A co-worker once proposed to me that "maybe the philosophers are right: what we call real and physical is an *illusion*." I asked what he meant by "an illusion." He said that maybe it was an illusion that a real physical world exists separate from our mind; the mind gives us only an illusion of material reality. I asked if he thought that this applied to our brains as well, since our brains are physical matter. He said it did. To this I asked: "If so, and we use our brains to think, wouldn't the thought that all reality is 'an illusion' be itself an illusion?"

We cannot say our brain, which produces real thoughts, can tell us that our thoughts are an illusion. To say "all is an illusion" implies that we know what *real* is. It is contradictory to say it is real that everything is an illusion. We cannot claim that "all is an illusion" is a true theory, because the theory itself would be an illusion. The theory proves itself to be false, because it is self-contradictory. Therefore, it is false that all things are an illusion.

Eastern religions have various terms, such as the Ultimate or the One, for what is understood as the ultimate reality in their pantheistic view. If the One is the source of everything, then the One is the source of what we perceive as reality. But if all is an illusion, then we have the contradictory view that the only reality is that everything is an illusion! In other words, it is contradictory to think that if everything is an illusion, I must exist to have this thought; but if my existence is an illusion, then how would I have this thought? It is like thinking that there is nothing to think about.

The One cannot simultaneously be the source of enlightenment and the source of ignorance and illusion, because that is contradictory. We would never know if we are enlightened or whether we're stricken with ignorance.

---

15. Quinn, "Pantheism," 677.

No One Lives Consistently with a Worldview of Illusion

Mystical New Age devotees influenced by Hindu ideas have told me that only the mind is real, our bodies are mere containers for the mind, the physical world is illusionary—imagined. To point out the contradiction in this view, I have asked them to imagine several scenarios:

Imagine you're rushed to the hospital with a cut artery, and the doctor offers you imaginary surgery and imaginary bandages. Or suppose you put in a week of work, and the boss says, "Here is your imaginary check."

I once attempted to hear a lecture by New Age religious sect leader Elizabeth Claire Prophet (1939-2009) of The Church Universal and Triumphant. At the entrance of the building, I spoke to one of her followers taking entry tickets. I asked him what he held as a core belief, now that he was a follower of Ms. Prophet. He said that reality is in the mind and that the physical world was an illusion.

I asked to go inside to listen to Ms. Prophet, but he refused me entrance because I did not have a ticket. I told him that I'm an illusion, so I'm not really standing in front of him; my body only appears to be here; therefore, it doesn't matter if I have a ticket, which ticket is also an illusion anyway. I asked him how he could assert this philosophy of illusion while simultaneously acknowledging that I really exist and demanding a real ticket from me. We either exist in reality or we don't. I cannot exist and not exist at the same time. Instead of discussing the contradiction, he said, "You cannot enter without a ticket." Neither he, nor Ms. Prophet, could live consistently with this worldview of illusion.

Your Wife Might Be an Illusion

A member of the Church of Christ, Scientist (the Christian Science religious view) and I were discussing Jesus's death and resurrection. He said that it only appeared that Jesus died and rose again because the physical world is not reality; only spiritual things of the mind are real. He said that Christian Science teaches that evil does not exist, that the body with sickness and handicaps only appears to be real; but the spiritual nature of people is more real—true reality.

I asked him if he was married, and he said that he was. I proposed that the next time he is alone with his wife in a romantic dinner setting that maybe she really wasn't there.

Sorting through Worldviews

I shared the biblical account of Jesus, which tells us that Jesus lived in a body; healed bodily sickness in people; and really suffered, died, and rose from the dead for the forgiveness of the evil of sin. It is Eastern mysticism to deny that sickness and death exist. Hospitals and funeral homes are not an illusion. Jesus's bodily resurrection confirmed that the body is real, as shown in Luke 24 when Jesus, after his resurrection, walked, talked, and ate with two men.

Mary Baker Eddy (1821–1910) is the founder of the Christian Science Church and wrote its primary book, *Science and Health with Key to the Scriptures*. Some of her major themes are that the physical world, including evil, is not real. She writes: "If God, or good, is real, then evil, the unlikeness of God, is unreal."[16] She asserts that "the notion that both evil and good are real is a delusion."[17] She speaks of the "illusion of sickness."[18] She says "that nothing possesses reality nor existence except the divine Mind and His ideas."[19]

A Pulitzer Prize-winning author, Caroline Fraser, wrote about how she came out from under the influence of the Christian Science Church. She says that, according to Eddy, "the material world . . . including death" are "an illusion" and "since God did not make our bodies, they do not exist."[20] Eddy's Christian Science view is anti-biblical. The nail prints in Jesus's hands (John 20:24–29) survived the resurrection, indicating the physical reality of the crucifixion and further indicating that he will never repeat it.

Yin and Yang Dualism and the Tao

Yin and *Yang* is a phrase of Chinese philosophy symbolized by:

This symbol illustrates the worldview of the equality of cosmic opposites, or "forces of a divided but complimentary universe."[21] Yin is the

---

16. Eddy, *Science and Health*, 470.
17. Eddy, *Science and Health*, 330.
18. Eddy, *Science and Health*, 495.
19. Eddy, *Science and Health*, 331.
20. Fraser, *God's Perfect Child*, 184.
21. Chan, "Orderly Realm of Chinese Sages," 124.

The Eastern Religious Worldview

large black area and symbolizes darkness, femininity, and passivity, among other concepts. Yang is the large white area and symbolizes light, masculinity, activity—the opposite of the Yin area. Within darkness, there is light (white dot), and within light, there is darkness (black dot). The entire circle symbolizes the eternal cycles of equal existence. A summary phrase of this Yin/Yang worldview is *dualism*. The Yin/Yang concept was initiated by Lao Tzu, a Chinese philosopher from about 500 BC. Lao Tzu speaks of the *Tao* as the "Great Ultimate" principle that produces the Yin and Yang.[22]

Taoist practitioner and author Solala Towler sums up this symbol as "representing the two primal forces of the universe," which are "opposites" that "complement each other."[23] Towler uses nature as a metaphor of Yin and Yang by pointing out that plants die, return to the earth, and sprout again, over and over. He says, "We, as humans, are also subject to these same laws of yin/yang" wherein we grow, die, and are "reborn again in another body, another life."[24]

Yin/Yang implies that good and bad are within all humans and are part of the eternal process. This leads to the concept that good and bad actions, such as justice/injustice, mercy/cruelty, with corresponding evil and suffering, are not real differences. They are just equalizing and balancing forces. If so, then there is no hope that, in the future, good will overcome evil. In contrast, the Bible reveals in Revelation 21 and 22 that evil and suffering will be overcome.

People who claim to be Taoist do not live as if the Yin/Yang philosophy, which asserts that there is no real distinction between good and evil, is really true. The following story shows a couple contradictions in the Taoist worldview philosophy.

In conversation with a man with this dualistic worldview and a Yin/Yang tattoo, I asked how this philosophy worked for him. He said that he tried not to be disturbed by events in life, all opposites like good and evil work together, and no one can really attain knowledge of this Ultimate principle. I recognized this as a Taoist worldview.

"Can we know the Tao, the Ultimate?" I asked.

He said, "The Tao is unknowable."

"But if so, how do you *know* this?" I asked.

---

22. Chan, trans., *Way of Loa Tzu*, 6.
23. Towler, *Tao of Intimacy and Ecstasy*, 11.
24. Towler, *Tao of Intimacy and Ecstasy*, 12.

I pointed out that it is contradictory to say that the Ultimate principle of the universe is unknowable, because it asserts what you know about this Ultimate unknowable principle.

"Is this Ultimate principle personal or impersonal?" I asked.

He said that it was personal.

I asked if that meant a personal God existed separate from the cosmos as its Creator. He said that God—the Tao—was not separate from the universe, so then he concluded that the Yin/Yang principle must be impersonal. I suggested that an impersonal Yin/Yang means that opposites like good/bad, mercy/cruelty are eternal and would have equal value, since one did not precede the other. There would be no objective distinction between goodness/evil or between mercy/cruelty. So I asked the man if he thought that doing something cruel to him is good. He said, "No." He made a distinction! No one can live in a world in which there is no distinction between cruelty and mercy.

Jesus's Victory Saves Us, Not Systems

Genesis 1, 2, and 3 give a non-pantheistic account of a cosmos by stating that God created everything, and these chapters also show that the personal God of heaven intended to be with the people on the earth. That is, heaven and earth came together. But this was corrupted by sin. Revelation 21 and 22 tells us of a "new *heaven* and a new *earth*" as a restoration of what was originally intended. The Bible starts and ends with creation as a place where God lives with humanity. Humanity does not merge with an impersonal God in a nonphysical realm of nirvana. The physical world is not divine, or relegated to inferiority, or denied reality, or seen as an illusion.

The Eastern religious pantheistic and karmic system means we live in a universe controlled by an impersonal cosmic or karmic system rather than by a personal God of love. An impersonal system cannot love us, and we cannot love a system. It is more reasonable to believe in a personal God coming to us in Jesus than it is to believe in an impersonal cosmic system.

Beware of the Eastern Religious Infiltration

Good biblical interpretive skills are needed to discern between Scripture and philosophical contradictions.

The Eastern Religious Worldview

When you read or hear of concepts using terms like karma; Nature (spelled with a capital N); the Universal One, or simply, the One; aligning with the frequency of the universe; sending out positive thoughts from your mind into the universe; or your words create reality—know that you're dealing with a New Age Hindu-like Eastern religious philosophy, not biblical thinking.

Positive thinking is a Christian value. However, if positive thinking is said to be the root cause of what is real, then you have moved into the Eastern religious worldview. Our imagination is a gift of God, but if we imagine unbiblical nonsense, then we have misused the gift.

15

The "All Ways Lead to God" Idea and Zen Buddhism

Dissecting the Self-Contradiction of Religious Pluralism

The Coffee Shop Napkin Example

WHILE SEATED AT A table in a coffee shop, a man next to me struck up a conversation that migrated to religious views. He said that all religions are basically the same, and all lead to God. I drew a diagram on a napkin and asked if it illustrated his view. It did, he said.

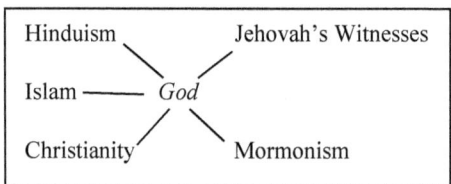

Which faith system is correct? They cannot all be true, because their truth claims are in contradiction to each other. In a contradiction of claims, one or more claims is false.

The "All Ways Lead to God" Idea and Zen Buddhism
Religious Pluralism Is a Contradiction

Pluralism is a popular modern worldview with Eastern religious roots. Pluralism means that all religions claims are valid *ways* to God and lead to the *same* God. Pluralism is another version of pantheism, because if God permeates all human views, then all views are equal. All beliefs are God's beliefs. Pluralism, by analogy, is like saying that it's the same electricity but lighting up different bulbs. This pluralistic claim, if true, should not lead to a contradiction. But it does. The contradiction shows up by a brief look at some examples of religious truth claims.

Hinduism. God did not create the universe, because God *is* the universe (pantheism).

Islam. Allah created the universe, which is a contradiction of Hinduism. Allah is not a Trinity and does not have a son.

Jehovah's Witnesses. God is not a Trinity, just as Islam claims; Jesus is the son of God, which is a contradiction of Islam; but the son was a created and non-divine being, which is a contradiction of Christianity.

Mormons. God has a body and became God from prior gods via an exaltation process, which is a contradiction of Islam and Jehovah's Witnesses.

Biblical Christianity. God is a Spirit who created the universe and is an eternal Trinity. Jesus is the uncreated and the eternal divine Son of God. This is a contradiction of the above-mentioned four religions.

It is reasonable to think that God would give a true revelation of himself, because he would know the truth about himself. But it makes no sense that God would reveal himself in contradictory ways. For example, God cannot be a Trinity and not a Trinity. Each person holding one of these views would defend their view as true but claim that an opposite view is false. This suggests that it cannot be true that all religious views are equally true.

I pointed out to this man that the pluralistic view that all religions views are all true and all lead to the same God is impossible, because these views are in contradiction to each other. If this is denied, then we have to settle on the irrational notion that God gives false views of himself.

His rebuttal was that we cannot rely on our reason to discuss God, because it destroys the transcendent mystery of God. But this statement itself purports to be reasonable. He was using reason to deny the use of reason, which is self-contradictory.

If God asserts contradictory views of himself, then God is not a truth-giver, and we would not know truth from error about God's nature.

Sorting through Worldviews

Zen Buddhism

Zen derives from a Chinese word for meditation. Zen is the ultimate pluralistic and subjective philosophy, because God, along with all religious views and doctrine, can be ignored as irrelevant. However, Zen pluralism will be seen as contradictory in the following observations.

D. T. Suzuki (1870–1966) was a university professor of Buddhism in Japan and in Western countries. In *An Introduction to Zen Buddhism*, Suzuki outlines Zen philosophy. The following selected comments are from this book.

"Personal experience . . . is everything in Zen."[1] "Enlightenment" in Zen is called *satori*, and "without it there is no Zen."[2] In order to attain *satori*, it is necessary to view logic as a "feature of Western thought" and view Zen as "illogical."[3] Suzuki calls Western rational thought "the tyranny of logic."[4]

Concepts such as "dust is rising from the ocean"; "listen to the sound of one hand" clapping; "the iron trees are in full bloom"; and to "see the stick" and not see a stick are examples of true Zen thinking.[5] Zen denies the existence of contradictions, so something can exist and not exist simultaneously.[6] Zen is the elimination of object and subject "where there are no antitheses [opposites]."[7] Note that all of this implies that whatever we can imagine, or conceive as nonsense, is Zen! This is a misuse of the imagination.

Suzuki says that "Zen has nothing to teach us in the way of intellectual analysis; nor has it any doctrine . . . for acceptance."[8] "No amount of . . . teaching . . . will ever make one a Zen master."[9] But we have to ask: aren't these statements actually doctrinal statements meant to teach us what Zen is? It's amazing that Suzuki wrote his book to teach us what Zen *is* while denying that Zen teaches anything.

---

1. Suzuki, *Introduction to Zen Buddhism*, 3.
2. Suzuki, *Introduction to Zen Buddhism*, 58, 65.
3. Suzuki, *Introduction to Zen Buddhism*, 5, 28.
4. Suzuki, *Introduction to Zen Buddhism*, 28.
5. Suzuki, *Introduction to Zen Buddhism*, 28–32.
6. Suzuki, *Introduction to Zen Buddhism*, 29.
7. Suzuki, *Introduction to Zen Buddhism*, 9.
8. Suzuki, *Introduction to Zen Buddhism*, 8.
9. Suzuki, *Introduction to Zen Buddhism*, 102.

The "All Ways Lead to God" Idea and Zen Buddhism

Suzuki mentions "the truth of Zen" while simultaneously saying that Zen has no objective doctrine of truth.[10] Suzuki cannot live consistently in the worldview that denies opposites. If Zen contains "ultimate truth,"[11] then there must be error—the opposite of truth.

In Zen, there is "no God to worship," because, in Zen, "God is neither denied nor insisted upon; only there is in Zen no such God as has been conceived by . . . Christian minds."[12] "Zen wants absolute freedom even from God."[13]

Suzuki's book ends with a quote from Matthew 6:1–6 that records Jesus saying that God will *reward or recompense* those whom he sees praying in "secret." Suzuki says that this is *not* in accordance with Zen, because "as long as there is any thought of anybody . . . knowing of our doing and making recompense, Zen would say, 'You are not yet one of us.'" Therefore, regarding this comment on prayer by Jesus, Suzuki says, "Zen will have none of it."[14] Zen disallows Jesus's teachings. Lastly, Suzuki says this about Christianity: "In Christianity we seem to be too conscious of God . . . Zen wants to have this last trace of God-consciousness . . . obliterated."[15]

Zen meditation attempts to eliminate all opposites, and in doing so it eliminates all sense of sin. Sin is the opposite of what an objective God's moral will is. This is why a Zen practitioner would sense inner peace: there is no annoying stir of moral guilt. Spiritual subjectivity relieves people from thinking in terms of real objective moral guilt and, as a result, eliminates the sense that we need forgiveness.

Zenists deny objective distinctions in religious views but then make a distinction between Christianity and Zen by rejecting Jesus's view regarding prayer to God, because it is contradictory to Zen. Zen is a claim of exclusivity, after all. This is contradictory to the basic premise that religious inclusivism is true. The end result of Zen is that there is no hope for salvation, since the need for it is eliminated in the Zen effort. Zen is anti-Christian, even if Zen philosophy is encased in Christian terms or concepts by teachers purporting to be Christians.

---

10. Suzuki, *Introduction to Zen Buddhism*, 28, 53, 65, 99.
11. Suzuki, *Introduction to Zen Buddhism*, 78.
12. Suzuki, *Introduction to Zen Buddhism*, 9.
13. Suzuki, *Introduction to Zen Buddhism*, 67.
14 Suzuki, *Introduction to Zen Buddhism*, 101.
15. Suzuki, *Introduction to Zen Buddhism*, 102.

Sorting through Worldviews

The Blind Men and the Elephant

To prove a pluralistic worldview is valid, an analogy of three blind men touching an elephant, which stands as a symbol of God, is sometimes offered to the Christian. One man touches the side of the beast and concludes, "It's a wall." Another touches a leg and says that it's a tree trunk; the third touches the tail and says it's a rope. All three have their perspective based on their sense experience, and all three are claiming what is true *for them*. See, the pluralist may say, all views are limited, but none are wrong. This is the pluralistic worldview that all religions have a limited view but are equally valid.

Observe, however, that, in the analogy, all three men are blind. Second, all three men are wrong. We know this, because we are not blind. We know they are touching a real elephant, not a wall, tree, or rope. All three conclusions about what the elephant actually is are contradictory. All conclusions are false as to the true nature of the elephant. The analogy sounds spiritual, but the analogy proves itself to be . . . a bad analogy.

What about the Cannibals?

A religious pluralist said to me that all religious views are valid. In response, I suggested the following scenario. Suppose you're in a pot of soup over a fire among a tribe of cannibals who are placing sliced carrots and celery into the pot, and you realize that you're the religious sacrificial dinner. Would you think, "This seems like a fine religious practice"? No pluralist would think that being the main course for dinner is a valid religious view among all other valid religious views. Religious pluralism cannot be maintained, because the pluralist eventually denies pluralism.

Truth Is Exclusive

The Eastern religious New Age concept asserts a pluralistic *all-inclusive* idea that all faiths are valid. However, Eastern religious views do not really accept all faiths as true. For example, Hinduism states that Christianity is wrong, because Christianity is not pantheistic. Buddhism denies the Hindu scriptures, called Vedas, as authoritative. Zen denies that religious dogma is relevant. This shows that Eastern religious devotees live in contradiction to their inclusivism.

The "All Ways Lead to God" Idea and Zen Buddhism

A woman said to me that she was not religious but was spiritual, and she was in the New Age mystical movement. She said that she accepted all religious beliefs as true.

I asked, "Do you think Christianity is true?"

"Yes, if that's your belief," she said.

"I think New Age philosophy is false. Am I right?"

"No. That's being exclusive. You're wrong to say that."

"But," I said, "you just said all belief systems are true. How can you now claim my belief that New Age is wrong, is a wrong belief?"

It is contradictory for a New Age mystic to assert that all religious beliefs are true and then say that a Christian is wrong, if we deny that New Age philosophy is true. Truth is by nature exclusive, because truth excludes that which is false. A false statement cannot, in fact, be true. We might like to imagine that all religious views are true, but we cannot live consistently within this inclusive system we imagine. The pluralist will eventually come upon a religious view they think is false. This stands in contradiction to pluralism.

Pluralism reduces all religious ideas down to a common level, as if spiritual truth were just an emanation of metaphysical communism.

16

God's Goodness vs. Evil and Suffering
If God Is Good, Then How Can There Be Evil and Suffering?

Evil and Suffering (ES) Defined

THIS CHAPTER BEGINS TO discuss a more pressing and practical matter of life: evil and suffering (ES). ES is used as an overarching description of all that is wrong with the world. When evil is used as a separate word in this chapter, it means *moral* evil against people and nature, such as crimes, tyranny, pollution, and so forth. When suffering is used separately, it means physical, mental, and emotional pain resulting from events like war, disasters, accidents, disease, and crimes. Dealing with an apparent incompatibility between God, as ultimately good and all-powerful, and the presence of ES is "the premier challenge to Christianity."[1]

The Pastoral/Comforting Approach vs. the Rational Approach

When I was a police officer, I went to a home where a young man had committed suicide with a handgun. He was lying in a bedroom. His distraught mother was seated at a table in the kitchen. I sat with her for about an hour

---

1. Oliphint, *Reasons for Faith*, 262.

God's Goodness vs. Evil and Suffering

while she cried and asked, "Why did this happen?" This was an emotionally driven question, not an academic one, so I did not offer rational answers on the problem of evil. Instead, I sat with her. I told her of God's love, that God understood the depression of her son, and that God understood her emotional agony. She needed someone to feel bad *with* her. This is the *pastoral* approach. During sorrow is not the time to offer rational explanations for tragedy. Never get the pastoral and rational approaches confused.

Paul writes that "in all things God works for the good" (Rom 8:28). This is not saying that all things themselves are good, or that God is the proximate—preceding or direct—cause of all things. For God to allow the possibility of ES is not the same as causing it.

Dealing with the Why Question

When tragedy and suffering strike us from a morally evil act such as a mass shooting, we want to know "Why did the shooter do this?" We ask this as if there were a rational answer. But if the shooter told us his reason, we would not say, "Well, that makes sense," because the act is without reason. Moral evil is the opposite of the rational nature of God.

When suffering results from a tragedy such as a heart attack, we ask the question why. This question enters a different realm, because the tragedy is not from a morally evil act. I will not attempt to answer the question of why any specific tragedy in life happens. Sad events in life happen. We have to support other people in the pastoral approach.

This chapter will deal only with the *origin*—the emergence—of ES in the world. That is, whom do we blame? We will investigate the rational aspect of ES in this sense: is the existence of real ES a valid argument against the existence of God?

Theodicy

This word comes from two Greek words: *theo* (God) and *dike* (judgment, right). A theodicy explains how ES cannot be used to contradict God's existence or criticize his nature.

Moral and Physical Depravity

The world's problems are a consequence of Adam's moral rebellion. That is, Adam's sin resulted in human moral depravity, which led to additional moral and physical problems. Adam brought *depravity* into existence. There are two kinds of depravity: moral and physical. For example, moral depravity is evidenced by man *a* hitting man *b* with a club; and physical depravity is evidenced by man *b* suffering a broken arm. Spraining a wrist from an accidental fall is another example of physical depravity.

Why doesn't God stop these circumstances before they happen? Or why not reverse the effects as if they never happened? It is because God allows human sin to have its consequences. God sometimes does intervene, and we call this grace, or a miracle.

What Kind of God Do You Reject?

When a God-skeptic states, "I don't believe God exists," we may ask what kind of God do you *not* believe in? The response is generally: the kind of God that allows ES. Some follow-up questions help clarify the skeptic's position: "Is the Holocaust an example of so much moral evil as an indication that God does not exist?" "Would you believe in God if there was less suffering in the world?"

These kinds of questions discern what a lot of evil, including various forms of suffering, really is and whether it's logical to argue that "so much suffering" proves God's nonexistence. We are asking if there is such a thing as a sum total of ES that would indicate God does not exist. If the objection to God is based on the *amount* of ES, then we might ask, "What about the amount of good acts?" Wouldn't good acts be evidence of God's existence, if one is looking at events as evidence? In the end, pointing to an implied sum of evil acts, with corresponding suffering, is not a solid argument for God-skepticism.

What if God Had a Bigger Plan?

I read the story of Polish military officer Witold Pilecki, who voluntarily assumed a fake identity and went into Auschwitz during World War II as part of a plan to report on the death camp to the underground resistance and to the Allied forces. He was in the camp for over two years. He saw many murders, some he could have stopped, but he did not stop them, because Pilecki and the resistance had a bigger plan to stop tens of thousands from being murdered.[2]

How does this relate to God and the origin of ES? If we say that a good God must prevent any evil when he can, what if he had some reason to not stop Adam's failure? Theologian Gregory Koukl says that "a good person might allow evil he could have prevented if he had a good reason to do so."[3] Koukl argues that if God had a reason to allow evil to come into existence because he had a good reason, then God is not obligated to have prevented it. The good reason God had was that God wanted humans in a free personal relationship, and, therefore, God allowed the possibility of ES through Adam, without being the cause of it. Norman Geisler puts it this way: "God is responsible for making evil possible, but free creatures are responsible for making it actual."[4]

Sin Defined

Stephen Davis and Eric Yang write that "sin is essentially . . . a state of being—a state of separation from God."[5] This is a state of being that perpetuates bad acts. That is, evil acts are evidence of our being sinners.

Sin is anything contrary to God's moral law, as in 1 John 3:4, which says "sin is lawlessness." Sin works towards destruction. To say God wanted sin to exist would imply that God wanted ES to exist. This leads to the contradictory notion that God willed to create a world with a simultaneous will for its demise, as if God were a maestro of devastation.

Andrew Schmutzer says, "Sin is anti-creational," as it is an assault on God's "relational eco-system."[6] Emil Brunner asserts that "sin spoils the creative work of God."[7]

---

2. Fairweather, *Volunteer*.
3. Koukl, *Story of Reality*, 89.
4. Geisler, *Baker Encyclopedia of Christian Apologetics*, 219.
5. Davis and Yang, *Introduction*, 109.
6. Schmutzer, in Peterman and Schmutzer, *Between Pain and Grace*, 51.
7. E. Brunner, *Revelation and Reason*, 66.

Sorting through Worldviews

Various False Assumptions Followed by Refutations

Inaccurate concepts of God are *assumed* by the skeptic, stemming from the fact that ES exists. Some assumptions as criticisms of God are as follows.

Assumption #1: God created ES, so God is not all-good.
Assumption #2: ES is proof that God does not exist.
Assumption #3: ES proves God is not all-powerful or all-loving.
Assumption #4: God could have made a better world.

The following are brief remarks in response to these criticisms.

To assumption #1, *God created ES, so God is not all-good*: this argument is theologically and logically incoherent.

The following show *theological contradictions*.

God hates wickedness/evil (Ps 45:7), but if he wills evil, then God wills what he hates. If so, we could not say anything was against the will of God.

If God has a simultaneous will for both good and evil, then God is morally dualistic. This is what the impersonal Yin/Yang cosmos looks like, where there is no chance that good eventually wins over evil. Dualism contradicts the Bible's claim that all suffering will end (Rev 22:1–5). If good and evil are equal, it does not matter which one we eliminate.

Jesus came to "destroy" the work of Satan (1 John 3:8 and Heb 2:14). But if ES is the will of God, then we arrive at the contradictory view that Jesus came to destroy the works of his Father. William Hasker states that "if we have no idea whatever of the sorts of things God can and cannot be expected to do, the notion that God is good . . . lacks all content."[8]

The following show *logical contradictions*.

If God is all-good, but does evil, too, evil would be good. This eliminates the distinction between good and evil, just like the Eastern religious concept that ES is an illusion. Murder, for example, would only appear as evil. Evil acts are preceded by thoughts, motives, and intentions. If acts are eternally determined in God's mind, then events and God would be without distinction, as in Hindu pantheism.

Furthermore, it is contradictory to think that God could create evil. John Stackhouse Jr. says that "evil is not a *something* that God could *create*," like a "molecule," because evil is "not a thing itself."[9] Evil is the corruption of preexisting goodness. For example, rust exists, because a good piece of iron preexisted. Metal can rust or not, so rust has *contingent* existence (does not

---

8. Hasker, *Triumph of God over Evil*, 121.
9. Stackhouse, *Can God Be Trusted?*, 41.

God's Goodness vs. Evil and Suffering

have to exist). Rust derives its existence from something else. Geisler states, "Rust is a corruption of a good thing (iron)," and "rust does not exist in and of itself. It is a privation or lack in a good thing ... Nonetheless, rust is real," as a "real lack in a good thing."[10] Louis Markos posits this analogy: "Evil is like a tear in a shirt; apart from the shirt itself, the tear has no existence."[11]

God's eternal nature is good, so goodness has eternal and necessary existence. Evil derives from the existence of preceding goodness. Pastor Timothy Keller puts it this way: "Evil is an intrusion into God's good creation."[12] The difference between *necessary* existence and *contingent* existence can be seen this way: God was not caused; God has to exist; therefore, he has necessary existence. The universe is a creation of God, but God did not have to create; therefore, the universe has contingent—not necessary—existence.

To assumption #2, *ES is proof that God does not exist*: actually, evil proves the opposite. Evil proves *that* God exists, because we would not know evil if there were not a preceding good. We know a crooked line, because a straight line is first necessary. If, for example, there were no such thing as necessarily real musical pitches, we would not know what singing off-key is.

To assumption #3, *ES proves God is not all-powerful or all-loving*: our misuse of moral freedom does not prove or even indicate a deficiency in the nature of God as all-powerful and all-loving.

A co-worker once stated to me that a particular school shooting would not have happened if there were a God.

I asked, "If in order to have a universe wherein evil did not come into existence, would you be willing to give up art, music, and inventions that improve life?"

He said that life would be boring without all of this.

I pointed out that without moral free will, the creative genius of artists like Monet, the music of Lennon and McCartney, the creativity of Bill Gates would never be actualized. We could not make distinctions between genius and grass growing. In fact, we would not be aware of love, since there would be no awareness of the moral distinction that is the root of loving relationships. Love is rooted in free will, and love would not exist if there were no possibility of making moral choices. Love would not arise between two

---

10. Geisler, *If God, Why Evil?*, 20.
11. Markos, *Apologetics*, 34.
12. Keller, *Walking with God*, 136.

trees or two tomato plants. To be human, we must be moral beings capable of moral choice between good and evil, and to give that up renders us less than human, and not morally responsible.

To assumption #4, *God could have made a better world*: if we think about what God "could have made," then we arrive at the reasonable conclusion that God made the exact world we really do want.

Another detective and I were sitting in my car waiting to execute a search warrant on a suspect's house. My friend said that the world had some bad people in it, and if God existed, God would have created a "better world" than this one. Without realizing it, my friend's comment was the best subject to show the authenticity of the creation stories in Genesis 1 and 2. It was like he was sitting on a gold mine without a shovel. I began to dig.

I asked, "Does it seem as if God could have done a better job in the beginning?"

"I think so," he said.

"Interesting," I said, "but let me ask you this. What alternative options did God have when creating a world in order to make it a better one?"

"I don't know," he responded.

I said, "Well, let's see. It seems like God had three options." I proposed that God did not have to create any world, but since he did, we should consider if it logically follows that God could have created a better world than the one we have.[13]

Option 1: Create a universe of objects without a moral nature. This is a universe of objects such as inorganic rocks or organic lizards that act robotically by instinct. A world of non-moral objects is not better than a world with moral beings capable of loving relationships.

Option 2: Create a world of humans but make it impossible to do evil. But a world in which free choice is impossible is robotic, so then creativity and love would not exist. Human robotic objects are not better than any other robotic object like lizards. This is the same as option 1 and is not a better world either.

Option 3. Create a world in which people can make moral choices. This is exactly the world people want, and it is the world described in Genesis 1 and 2. God-skeptics and Christians share the same biblical view. This shows that the Bible is not disconnected from how people think. This option gives us a world in which real loving relationships exist, and this is better than any other world.

---

13. I learned this concept from Geisler, *If God, Why Evil?*, 57–69.

My friend said that he saw no other option beyond the third one.

"Better"

The term *better* implies that there is real and ultimate good in the universe; otherwise, the term makes no sense. When we ask for a better world in which evil does not exist, we are appealing to a standard of ultimate goodness in which this world falls short. If morals are only a matter of human preference, then morals are mere opinions. But who reasonably decides what is morally better? Hitler? Stalin? The majority vote? Human reason is insufficient for moral absolutes. A transcendent God is the only reasonable option for moral absolutes.

In Alvin Plantinga's Free Will Defense argument, Plantinga says that beings who are morally "free" to do good or evil are "more valuable . . . than a world containing no free creatures at all."[14] In other words, there would be no real freedom if God removed moral will, because it would be a world no better than a robotic world, as in options 1 and 2 above.

Starting at the Beginning with Adam as the Origin of ES

Theologian Frank Turek sums up Genesis 1, 2, and 3 by stating that "Christianity traces all of our trouble back to the freewill choice of Adam. As a result, we live in a fallen, broken world where bad things happen."[15] Adam and Eve lost spiritual access to God, incurred guilt, and came under the influence of selfishness; and the earth was affected as well.

God determined that Adam would have *moral sovereignty*—the final choice to obey God or not. Adam used his good gift of moral consciousness wrongly. Turek says, "God allows evil to respect our free choices."[16] We use good gifts wrongly every day. I may use the good gift of speech wrongly by hurling hate-speech to someone. We are responsible for our free moral decisions, even if such decisions are influenced by our past or some other factor. Our free will is not out of a vacuum. Paradoxically, I am free to choose but constrained to selfishness. None of this is God's fault.

---

14. Plantinga, *God, Freedom, and Evil*, 29–31.
15. Turek, *Stealing from God*, 129.
16. Turek, *Stealing from God*, 141.

Sorting through Worldviews

Christians and non-Christians agree on this point: evil should not exist. The atheist assumes that if God exists, he would have created a good world without ES. God did just that, according to Genesis 1. The atheist actually affirms the biblical narrative that God originally created a good world, but humans corrupted it voluntarily. Ecclesiastes 7:29 confirms this by saying "God made humankind upright, but they have sought many evil schemes" (NET). Regarding Adam and Eve, Clay Jones states, "It is impossible to give beings free will and not allow them to use it wrongly—that's as logical as it gets."[17]

What if God Started with You?

One of my police officer friends told me that if God existed, then all of the suffering from crimes we see would not exist. I asked, "Are you saying that if God exists, he would dislike evil and would stop what he dislikes?"

She said, "Yes."

"Okay," I said, "but what if God started with you? What if he stopped you from doing anything he disliked? How would you like all this interference with your choices?"

"I'd probably get upset," she said.

"Exactly. You'd tell God that he was a cosmic meddler and to leave you alone."

This is similar to saying that she wanted God to interfere, just as long as he didn't interfere with her. This is like a motorist telling a police officer, "Go away and do your job; just don't do it on me and write out that speeding ticket."

Atheists and Christians agree: evil comes from humans. New Testament scholar N. T. Wright states: "The problem of evil . . . is . . . a problem about me."[18]

Natural Evil

This term refers to destructive events of nature like disease, floods, hurricanes, which cause suffering. Evil in this context means bad events not directly caused by immoral acts. How do we explain that nature causes

---

17. Jones, *Why Does God Allow Evil?*, 207.
18. Wright, *Evil and Justice*, 97.

suffering without blaming God for it, since he created nature? Theologically, we have to start in Genesis 1, which states that all of creation was "good." Genesis 2 states that Adam and Eve were to be the caretakers of the world. Genesis 3 shows that Adam and Eve disobeyed, and as a consequence, sin affects nature. This is implied from Romans 8:18–25 ("creation . . . will be liberated from its bondage to decay"). These verses in Romans show that the original creation was not intended to suffer decay or cause suffering.

I might ask, "God, why'd you let me break my leg when I tripped?" The answer: gravity and concrete. Jones observes that "natural laws must work in regular ways."[19] In other words, we suffer from mishaps, which are not God's fault. God lets the natural world work according to natural laws. Natural evil is not proof that God does not exist.

Moral and natural evil operate as a dysfunction of the originally good world. Thomas Schreiner points out that because of Adam's failure, "creation has not fulfilled the purpose for which it was made."[20] But when all of humanity's full redemption is realized, Schreiner says, "The return of nature to its purpose will coincide" with human freedom from sin and its consequences.[21]

There is an underlying yet incorrect assumption in affirming that for God to be God, God should have prevented natural disasters from even starting. In other words, we demand that for God to be seen as God, we must have a world as we like it. But God is not my servant.

Infant Suffering

The God-skeptic may argue that infant suffering is evidence that God does not exist, because, if he did, he would not allow it; or that God is not good, even if he does exist. We might ask the skeptic: should children be exempt from suffering? And, if so, at what age does this exemption expire? In other words, if God's existence is objected to by the skeptic based on infant suffering, is the skeptic arguing that suffering can begin at a later age? This question logically follows the objection.

Infants suffer things like disease and skinned knees. These kinds of sufferings are not directly caused by infants, as if the infants did something bad. Infants suffer because they are humans. I make this point about infants

---

19. Jones, *Why Does God Allow Evil?*, 113.
20. Schreiner, *Romans*, 436.
21. Schreiner, *Romans*, 437.

suffering resulting from being humans only to refute the accusation that their suffering shows that God does not exist or is inconsistent with a good God, if he does exist. This is the *rational* approach to the question, not the *pastoral* approach. Infant suffering affects our emotions, and it should. It should also prompt society to pastorally protect children from harm and to pray for God's intervention in healing.

An Insufficient Moral Reason for Evil Is a Claim of Omniscience

A skeptic told me, "There is no reason for much of the suffering in the world." I asked him how he would *know* this. He offered no answer. He did not know how he came to "know" this. Ronald Nash says that the argument that God has no reason for allowing ES is a claim of "omniscience" (all-knowledge), which the atheist does not have.[22]

A Revelation of God's Nature Does Not Depend on Its Opposite

"God wanted humans to see him as compassionate, so he decreed sin, evil, and suffering," a woman told me.

I asked, "Are you saying that God's good nature is revealed by its opposite, evil?"

"Well," she said, "we would not know Jesus as Savior without sin for him to save us from."

This argument is like saying that a heart surgeon wants me to have a heart attack so he can show himself to be a great surgeon. A revelation of God as a good and loving Savior cannot depend on evil. God does not need sin to prove anything about his nature. Suffering is not necessary for us to know sympathy, because that makes sympathy dependent on suffering. God is eternally loving and sympathetic; he does not need evil to prove it.

God Watches Over Even the Unbeliever

The World War II Japanese Commander Mitsuo Fuchida organized and led the Japanese surprise aerial attack of several hundred planes on Pearl

---

22. Nash, "Problem of Evil," 220.

Harbor in 1941. He is the one who broadcast "Tora, Tora, Tora" to his superiors as a confirmation that the Japanese surprise attack had succeeded. He became a Christian in 1950 and later came to live in America. In chapter 7 of his memoirs, he tells a story that took place in 1930, when he was a lieutenant on board a plane over the Taiwan Strait searching for a man lost at sea. The plane eventually had only ten minutes of fuel left. He said that he heard "somebody whisper" several times to him to "increase the altitude." He told the pilot to ascend, but the pilot refused because ascending uses up fuel. After Fuchida persisted, the pilot increased altitude. Then the fuel ran out. Fuchida said that their increased altitude allowed them to glide farther than they would have been able to glide if they were lower, and as a result, the plane glided close to a ship before the plane crashed in the ocean. The ship's crew rescued Fuchida and the pilot. Fuchida said later, after his conversion to Christianity, "It was the voice of Jesus, who ushered me to safety long before I recognized Him."[23]

Fuchida's story illustrates the common grace of God for all people. This is shown in a statement by Jesus, that God "makes his sun rise on the evil and on the good, and sends rain on the just and on the unjust" (Matt 5:45 ESV).

How God Deals with Moral Evil

The Gospel stories of Jesus do not include answers to solve the problem of evil in detail. Instead, God dealt with the problem personally in the work and ministry of Christ. In the Christlike pastoral model, when people are hurting, logical solutions to the problem of suffering, as I have mostly dealt with herein, do not directly apply. We should have answers to objections; however, we need to know that people are primarily in need of our comfort and support before they need our logical answers.

---

23. Fuchida, *For That One Day*, 35–40.

17

Salvation Is Not by Personal Merit

Discerning Whether Humans Must Earn Merit with God

A Discussion at Midnight

WHILE I WAS STANDING outside with a friend about midnight, the friend mentioned that his wife was starting to attend church, and this was disturbing to him. He believed in God but did not want to attend a church. The conversation moved to having a relationship with God. He said, "I am a good person," and he thought that was enough.

I asked him, "What would you say to the Lord if he asked you why he should allow you into heaven?"

"I'd say, 'I tried to do the right thing, and was a good person.'"

"How many good deeds would you need to do, as a daily average, to gain merit for heaven?" I asked.

After some discussion, we settled, hypothetically, on twenty good deeds per day. I proposed a scenario. Suppose you're standing at the gates of heaven and offered God your twenty good deeds per day accomplishment as a basis for God to allow you entrance to heaven. But suppose that God said the daily average amount was twenty-one, so you missed heaven by being short one good deed per day. Then I asked, "What would you say?"

He hesitated and then said that he would be in trouble.

I told him to look at the stars. I asked him if God would be impressed with our goodness, if God created the universe. We agreed that we could not live long enough to do enough good deeds to impress God, since we have already proved to God that we cannot be consistently good.

The problem with reliance on our goodness is that there is no way to know how good "good" is. We judge ourselves by our own standard, much like a child who is told to clean the bathroom but never gets to the corners, then states that the room is clean. When I present myself as the standard of goodness to qualify for heaven, I am presenting an already flawed product. Since I am the problem, how can I offer myself as the solution? Author Ray Beeson confirms the dilemma of trying to do the best you can to earn salvation by posing this question: "What is best?" Then Beeson explains that we have "no standard for measurement" to determine "whether or not we have been good enough."[1]

My friend and I concluded that there is no solution humanly possible. I asked if it seemed more reasonable to believe that God would deal with the sin personally. He thought that was the only solution. However, I pointed out, God was in heaven, so to deal with sin personally, God would need to be human. Enter Jesus.

I proposed that sin must be very bad if the only person in the universe who could deal with it was God. My friend said that this appeared true and that he had never thought of himself and God in this way before. I suggested that he talk with his wife. A month later, he told me that he had begun going to church with his wife.

Earning Merit with God by Good Works on a Plane Trip

On a plane flight, I sat next to a woman, and we discussed our religious beliefs. I asked her if she had a view of religion and if she attended a place of worship. She said that she was a Christian and believed that Jesus was both God and man, the Savior of the world, who died for us. But she said that she was frustrated over TV preachers who claim that if people say a prayer, then they will be saved. She thought if people want to be saved, they need to do good works. I asked if she thought that doing good works is earning merit that leads to salvation. She said it did, and "just asking Jesus into your heart was too easy."

---

1. Beeson, *Real Battle*, 195.

I asked if she thought that her good works were sufficient for heaven. She responded that she hoped so but was not sure. I agreed that it would make no sense for someone to say they knew they were saved, if salvation were contingent on doing good works, because it is not possible to know how good one has to be to be "good."

She clung to the argument that good works were necessary for salvation, so I asked, "Doesn't that imply that what Jesus did on the cross was *insufficient* for salvation?" I mentioned that when Jesus was hanging on the cross he said, "It is finished" (John 19:30), meaning all the work of salvation was finished. Jesus did not say, "My work is finished, and now you have to do your part." If we have to do our own good works to be saved, then "It is finished" means nothing.

I said, "Let me get your opinion on something. If Jesus was divine, and died on the cross for us, how could the work of divinity be insufficient for our salvation? That is, why would Jesus even need to die, if I can get to heaven by my own works?" This fine lady sat in silence for a moment, then said that she did not know how to answer these questions but would think about it.

The New Testament states that people who accept Christ as Savior have eternal life, as in John 3:16. It is contradictory to think that God's gift of eternal life is something that can be attained by temporal works in a finite lifetime. Note that eternal life is not borrowed life, as if God loaned us his life to see if we're good enough to keep it. We do not become saved or stay saved by good works. Good works are a response to grace, not a cause of it.

Using Human Attributes to See What God Is Like

While we were discussing God's characteristics, a friend asked how I would know what God is like. I said that we can consider some self-evident truths of God's nature by thinking about what humans possess. I asked if it made sense to think that, if humans can see, then God can see, too. He thought so. He also agreed with me that it makes sense to think that God can hear and communicate, since people hear and communicate. The conversation moved to love. Love in humans implies that God possess the moral quality of love. It is evident that human love reflects God's love and shows that God loves all humans. A relationship with God is rooted in his love towards us, not in our effort towards him. God loves to save souls and does so by grace.

Salvation Is Not by Personal Merit

God Is Not a Moral Accountant

God does not set up a moral accounting system at our birth to see if we make more deposits by good acts than fewer withdrawals by bad acts and then decide if we go to heaven when we die. This merit/debit concept eliminates the need for Jesus, because the accounting system implies that I can go to heaven based on my positive balance in a merit bank. Jesus paid the debt for all moral guilt, so we trust him for salvation, not ourselves.

Not Enough Time to Be Good Enough

During a discussion about salvation, two Jehovah's Witnesses admitted that they believed salvation depends on good works to some degree. "Well, let's see how this might work," I said. I looked at my watch and asked, "Suppose you have thirty seconds to live but really need sixty seconds to do additional good works. Is this okay for you?" I looked at my watch again and waited for their answer. Silence, accompanied by foot shuffles, ensued. After thirty seconds, I said, "Time's up." I explained that the concept of doing good works for salvation is logically flawed, because there is no way to know if you have enough time to earn it. If salvation is not by grace, then there is no other way to know God.

18

Absolutes vs. Relativism

The Case for Universal, Objective, and Absolute Truth

The Essence of Relativism

Relativism asserts that truth is "only relative to the individual or group holding [a truth claim] to be true."[1] In other words, there is no universal and objective truth applicable to all humans for all time; instead, moral truth is determined privately and individually. Relativism is a major worldview, so this chapter will deal with the implications of the view in order to see its inherent contradictions.

A Moral Standard Is Necessary for Moral Objectivity

I was talking to a non-Christian woman who was applying painted artwork onto a canvas. She said her art was an expression, and I could interpret it any way I want.

I asked, "Your artwork makes no statement or has a specific message?"

"No, it's personal to the viewer."

---

1. Birkett, "Relativism," 604.

I saw this as an opportunity to talk about Christianity, so I asked, "Like moral values, for example? Moral truth is whatever a person interprets to be right for himself or herself?"

"Yeah," she said as she applied more red paint.

"Do you think there are some acts that are really right or wrong that apply to all humans? Like stealing would be wrong?"

She said that it is "wrong to steal."

"I'm curious . . . what *standard* are you using to base your values of what is right or wrong?"

"Well, everyone knows stealing is wrong," she said.

"Yes, but how do we *know* this? Maybe God tells us this."

She said, "Don't need God. We know what is right or wrong."

The conversation continued to an example I gave of what a standard for knowing what right and wrong means. Philadelphia's objective existence acts as a standard to judge all descriptions of it; otherwise, any description is valid. God created us and gave us his moral nature; otherwise, morals are just an opinion reducible to what we like or dislike. Liking something becomes the criteria, which is not really a universal standard. This woman appealed to a moral standard that she correctly assumed I also had. The fact that we agreed on what was universally right and wrong showed an objective moral standard, which only God can provide.

When I suggested—hypothetically—that red paint can be interpreted as "killing people for fun is okay," she rejected this interpretation of her art. But if interpretation is a private matter, how can it be said that this opinion of what red paint means is wrong? The relativistic artist did not agree that I can interpret her art any way I want. Furthermore, her statement that her artwork does not have a specific message is itself a statement of her artwork. In other words, while denying her artwork made a statement, she continued to paint as a statement of what her art is supposed to state. It would be like saying, "My art conveys the message that there is no message to my art." This is contradictory. A relativist cannot live consistently in their relativistic worldview.

Universal, Objective, and Absolute Moral Values

The term *universal* means everywhere in the universe, *objective* means outside of human opinion, and *absolute* means eternal (not temporal or changing). Therefore, the phrase universal, objective, moral absolutes means that morals apply everywhere in the universe, are timeless, and are based in God. An evil act on a Monday in March, for example, is still evil on a Saturday in December. Real objective morals do not change according to geography or the calendar.

Either moral values are rooted in a universally objective moral Being or they are not. Without God, moral issues are not objectively real; they are just a collection of subjective personal opinions. Some people may believe a specific act is wrong, but the act cannot be shown as objectively wrong. To be universally, objectively, and absolutely wrong, we must go outside of the cosmos to an infinite moral Being: God.

Killing for Fun

If a moral act is *universally* wrong, then it is wrong everywhere at all times. It would be wrong in Pittsburgh and wrong in the Andromeda Galaxy. A moral act that is objectively wrong means that it is wrong regardless of my opinion of the act.

Who determines moral absolutes? Not an individual, because an individual is not big enough to create absolutes for a society. Not a society, because a society is not big enough to create absolutes for a country. Not a country, because a country is not big enough to create absolutes for the world. Without God—the infinite moral Being—then no universal, moral, absolute standard exists.

Atheists may agree that killing someone for fun is universally wrong but have no grounds for this view *as a universal*; it is only something they dislike. But where did atheists get this sense of a universal moral principle? They have a universal moral sense but do not know where it came from.

When discussing moral relativism with someone, I bring up an example. "If relativism is true, then maybe torturing someone for fun is wrong on Earth but could be right in another galaxy. What do you think?" I receive "maybe" as the most common relativistic answer. So then I ask, "But . . . what if you're visiting that planet, and they want to torture your own child for fun? Is that okay?" This is not okay to the relativists. This shows that at least one act is considered universally wrong. How is that possible in relativism? A relativist cannot live consistently in relativism, because, eventually, relativism is denied.

Absolutes vs. Relativism

Atheists Don't Realize Why They Know Goodness Exists

When I told an atheist that God is the only ground for universal morals, he said this is absurd, because he believed in moral values, even though he was an atheist. He told me that we don't need a universal God to know that some act is wrong. He said, "You think that unless a person believes in God, that person cannot be 'good.'" I submitted that this is not what I was saying.

Michael Martin, a prominent atheist, implies that a believer in God thinks that atheists believe that there is no purpose or value to human life.[2] Christians, however, do not claim that atheists deny human purpose and value. We are saying that, without God, there is no *transcendent* basis for purpose and value; that the denial of God simultaneously denies an objectively universal basis to make a distinction between good and evil. We do not think that, in order to be good, you have to believe in God. As Christians, we can explain that the idea that an act is real and objectively good or evil is because of an objective personal God who created humans with moral intuitions.

Atheistic Evolutionists Live as If Morals Are Not Relative

Greg Epstein, the humanist chaplain for Harvard and M.I.T., says, "Our history began with the Big Bang" and developed from there, and "this is the story of evolution."[3] Epstein argues that morality is not "eternally objective."[4]

Scientist Richard Dawkins makes the argument that our roots in morality come from the evolutionary process of natural selection wherein genes select what favors survival.[5] Philosophy professor Richard Joyce's book is devoted to the entire theme of how morality evolved.[6]

Consider that people are either moral beings because of a transcendent God or not. If not, then morals are not transcendent and must have naturalistically evolved. But why did morals evolve? For the atheist, morals are a construct of evolutionary natural selection, because ethical living works towards surviving in society. The atheist senses universal morals but catapults them into the opposite realm of the sociological survival of the

---

2. M. Martin, *Atheism*, 13–24.
3. Epstein, *Good without God*, 8.
4. Epstein, *Good without God*, 35.
5. Dawkins, *God Delusion*, 241–67.
6. Joyce, *Evolution of Morality*.

fittest. Then, astonishingly enough, atheists live as if morals are transcendent, as they assert some acts are universally wrong! Without realizing it, atheists show evidence of God by seeing that universal, objective morals are real.

Moral Motivations in Atheists Proves God's Existence

While I was a detective, I was part of a team investigating financial elder abuse cases. This team included some atheists I knew. If morals are relative, why not defraud an elder? Because it's unfair? But this implies an objective standard of fair/unfair. If survival of the fittest is the mechanism for advancement in an environment, then financially defrauding a weaker elder advances the environment of the stronger defrauder. But an atheist friend in the team objected to financially defrauding weaker elders. Atheists live as if real objective moral values exist, in contradiction to the relativistic theory that the fittest survive over the weakest in their environment.

I submit the following conclusion. The subjective feeling of moral motivations within atheists towards treating people fairly proves that there is a universal, objective, moral standard of goodness as absolute, and not from just an opinion of moral relativism. The feelings and actions of atheists show that something else exists in the universe beyond materialism—something metaphysical.

Purpose, Meaning, and Significance

A mindless origin of the cosmos means that there is no real objective meaning to life outside of materialistic survival of the genes. It is fruitless to ask what the meaning of life is. In a purely materialistic view of our origin, we cannot logically conclude that there are real moral values, because there is no objective basis for these values.

Denying God's Existence Denies Moral Absolutes

When a person denies the existence of an objective moral Being, judgment between ultimate moral truth and error is impossible, which results in the following notion: what I believe is true for me, and what you believe is true for you. This is contradictory in this sense: if I assert that someone's belief in relativism is wrong, and the person defends that relativism by stating that I am wrong, then the person is asserting that some beliefs are true and some are not. This is the opposite of relativism. If the relativist cannot live consistently in the worldview of relativism, then this worldview needs to be rethought.

Real Evil as a Corruption of Real Good

My wife and I visited the Auschwitz-Birkenau death camp on a trip to Poland. No one can stand in this death camp and deny that evil is objectively real. Auschwitz stands as a model for objective evil. If real objective evil exists, then real objective moral truth does, too. The perpetrators of Nazism's evil at Auschwitz emerged from a contingent of previously good and moral Germans who, for example, loved their families, pets, flowers, and theater. We accuse them of being inhuman. Actually, in Clay Jones's words, "Those who do genocide are not inhuman monsters—they're all too human. They are precisely human. Genocide is what the race of Adam does."[7]

Jones argues for the concept that evil does not spontaneously emerge; it comes out of preexisting normalcy that becomes corrupted. Jones quotes Holocaust survivor Fred E. Katz as saying, "Ordinary people, like you and me" participated in the Holocaust by actively killing people or by support thereof.[8]

In order to illustrate Jones's comments, I offer two examples of good and ordinary people becoming extremely corrupt. The first is from Simon Wiesenthal who is famous for his work in identifying Nazi war criminals. Wiesenthal was in a Nazi camp at a particular ghetto during World War II. He tells of Nazi SS Lieutenant Richard Rokita. Prior to the war, Rokita was a violinist. While overseeing prisoners, Rokita was obsessed with forming a musical band consisting of camp prisoners. Wiesenthal describes Rokita as a man "who daily slaughtered prisoners from sheer lust for killing, [and] had at the same time only one ambition—to lead a [musical] band," so Rokita ordered a prisoner to compose a "death tango," and when "the band played this tune, the sadistic monster Rokita had wet eyes."[9] That someone could move from being an ordinary person to a war criminal is an example of the corruption of goodness by evil ideology.

7. Jones, *Why Does God Allow Evil?*, 48.
8. Jones, *Why Does God Allow Evil?*, 60.
9. Wiesenthal, *Sunflower*, 12.

Sorting through Worldviews

The second example is from Henry Gerecke, a Lutheran minister who was sent to Nuremberg Prison after World War II in order to minister to the Nazi war criminals awaiting trial. His story is told by Tim Townsend in his book, *Mission at Nuremberg*. In regards to the Nazi criminals, Townsend says that Gerecke "strived to remember that before their [the Nazi criminals] alliance with Hitler, before the choices they made that led to mayhem and murder, they had all been boys once."[10] Gerecke's story shows that the evil ideas and deeds of these war criminals did not spontaneously appear; in fact, the criminals were once average people.

It reasonably follows that if there are actions regarded as universally and objectively evil, then real universal objective goodness must have preexisted. Evil derives its existence from eternal goodness. If this is denied, then what the Nazis did is merely something we don't like, not objectively evil.

Nazism proves that real evil exists and simultaneously proves real objective good exists. The argument that morals are relative is proven false by the assertion that the Nazis were really evil.

Fast Food and Moral Law

I was sitting in a restaurant booth drinking a milkshake near a man sitting in an adjacent booth who was reading the newspaper. He began a conversation about unethical people and that certain acts should be illegal. I agreed but said individuals, like us, cannot state what is illegal simply because we don't like a certain act. "Some acts," I said, "have been deemed illegal by the state legislature and codified in a penal code." He said he understood this concept of criminal law.

I asked, "What about moral law?" I explained that I was asking this to see if it made sense that, if there is criminal law against acts by a legislature, did it also make sense to think moral laws against lying or cheating, for example, come from a moral Lawgiver? In other words, without a moral Lawgiver, why do we think lying and cheating would be wrong? I admitted to him that I feel guilty about some unethical thought or act and asked if he had the same sensation of guilt on occasion. He did.

I asked, "What do you do with your guilt?"

"What do you mean?" he asked.

I proposed that my feeling of guilt stems from a violation of a real moral law and that this is only because there is a moral Lawgiver.

---

10. Townsend, *Mission at Nuremberg*, 141.

"Like God?"

"Yes, exactly," I responded.

I moved to his booth. I explained that God is the moral governor of the universe; we have violated his moral principles; and only God could rectify our guilt and did so in Jesus Christ. After some discussion, I asked if he would like to pray, ask for forgiveness, and invite Jesus into his life. He said he did, so we prayed. He had tears in his eyes and said he "never felt this way before." I put him in contact with a local pastor for follow-up.

All Ethical or Moral Truth Cannot Be Relative

A popular relativistic notion for moral values may be something like this: Ethical truth is valid for me if what I do does not harm others. But note that "not harm others" is the objective standard. Who determined this as a standard? This appeals to an objective moral standard, in contradiction that objective standards don't exist!

If it is asserted that universal truth does not exist, you might ask the person making this claim: should everyone believe this and be a relativist? If the relativist says yes, then this asserts the notion of universal truth, which is exactly what the relativist denies. In other words, the statement "All people should be relativists" claims relativism should be universally believed, while denying there is a universal truth to believe in.

If all truth is relative, the relativist has no grounds to expect me to convert. If all truth is relative, my truth—that relativism is wrong—is just as true as the relativist's argument that all is relative. This worldview of relativism is incoherent and cannot be lived out consistently.

Suppose a relativist claims that all moral truth is relative. Observe that this statement has meaning only if the statement itself is not relative. That is, it has meaning only if the statement is universally true. But relativism denies universal and objective truth. The statement is, therefore, without meaning.

Relativism Is Inconsistent and Self-Refuting

Relativism should show itself as a consistent worldview if it is the true worldview. But it cannot. Relativism always breaks down, because relativists eventually deny their own worldview. Here are some examples.

The bank manager. Suppose a relativist goes to his bank to withdraw money from an account and is told by the bank manager, "Your truth is that the money is yours, but my truth is that it is my money, so I withdrew the money and spent it." No relativist bank customer would accept this, because the relativist demands financial moral absolutes from bankers.

Medicine, marriage, court, and airplanes. No relativist patient would accept the act of a relativistic surgeon who said to the patient: "Even though it was your truth that you needed your gall bladder removed, I amputated your left leg, because it was my truth that your leg needed to be removed instead." A relativistic woman would not marry a man who gave his vows as "I promise to be relatively faithful to you." A relativistic juror in court would not like to hear a witness swear to "tell the relative truth and nothing but the subjective truth." And relativist passengers on a plane would revolt if the relativist pilot announced that even though the passengers' truth was that the flight was going to Chicago, the pilot's truth was that they were all going to Miami instead.

People profess relativism in their own lives but inconsistently demand absolutism from others. No one can live consistently in a world in which subjective ideas of truth prevail. This indicates that relativism is not a valid worldview.

Asking the Right Questions to Relativistic Statements

Learning to ask the right kinds of questions reveals that the relativist's *statement* cannot meet its own standard; therefore, the statement is self-refuting. Consider how to respond to the following relativistic statements.

There is no real perspective of truth. Ask: doesn't this statement claim a real, true perspective?

There is no one-true-belief system to believe by faith. Ask: should everyone believe this? If so, isn't this a one-true-belief system? This statement denies a one-true-belief system and then claims to be a one-true-belief system.

There is no ultimate truth. Ask: is this ultimately true for everyone? If so, then there *is* ultimate truth. If everyone should believe this, then the claim denies relativism.

There are no absolutes. Ask: are you absolutely sure? No one can logically say it's absolutely true that no absolute truth exists.

Nothing can be known for certain. Ask: do you know this for certain? The statement refutes its own premise of uncertainty.

The pursuit of ultimate truth is an illusion. Ask: wouldn't this concept also be an illusion?

Christians are judgmental and should not tell people they're wrong. Ask: is this your judgment? The statement is itself a judgment. If Christians are judgmental and intolerant when we say someone's worldview is wrong, wouldn't the relativist be judgmental and intolerant to claim that Christians are wrong?

In two books, Stuart Hackett discerns contradictions in relativism. He says that if a relativist claims that there are no objective truth judgments, then "the relativist is making the very sort of objective value claim" which is the very "doctrine" he or she "claims to be false."[11] Hackett explains that it is contradictory to claim that all ethical judgments are true only for the person making the judgment, because this claim really asserts what is true for all people. That is, the relativist asserts that it is universally and objectively true that ethical judgments are personally subjective. Therefore, Hackett says: "Consequentially, it turns out that if relativism is taken as objectively true," then relativism denies "its own assertion—which is self-contradictory."[12]

Os Guinness, a thoughtful and careful thinker, says that "there are some thoughts that can be argued but not lived."[13]

Four-Way Separation as Evidence That Goodness Went Wrong

There is evidence that things are not as they should be. Consider that we experience evidence of our separation from a rightly run world in four areas.

- From *God*, as evidenced by religious conflicts
- From *each other*, as evidenced by wars, crimes, and riots
- From *ourselves*, as evidenced by mental illness and suicide
- From the *world*, as evidenced by floods, pollution, and disease

If *evidence* is important to show that there is ultimate truth, then these examples show that something is wrong; thus, there must be some objective standard from which we all have fallen.

We should see the imperfections in people as evidence that there is real moral perfection in a transcendent Being. It's like seeing a pile of math tests wherein all of the students incorrectly answered the question of the

---

11. Hackett, *Recovery of Highest Good*, 100.
12. Hackett, *Resurrection of Theism*, 237–38.
13. Guinness, "Time for Truth," 49.

sum of two apples plus two apples as five. This imperfection of math suggests perfection in math; a real correct sum exists. In metaphysics, we call this perfection God.

Becoming a Better Person Is Impossible in Moral Relativism

Francis Beckwith and Gregory Koukl state that, logically, relativists cannot really "become better people," because to get better "implies an objective rule of conduct as the standard," which objective standard relativists deny. Relativists may change their behavior, but "if morals are entirely relative . . . then no way of thinking is better than another."[14]

When we see that we do not act as we should, then something is objectively wrong. But if there is no objective right, then how can we say anything is wrong? We do not live in a cosmic machine in which humans merely act out their genetic predispositions. Authors Nancy Pearcey and Charles Thaxton state that "the idea of improving one's life cannot occur to people trapped in a . . . deterministic view."[15]

Trying to become morally better contradicts moral relativism. To claim that everyone *ought* to be or *should* be a relativist is itself a contradiction of relativism, because there is no universal *ought* in relativism. The argument defeats itself by claiming what it denies.

The next chapter will help us see the moral implications of relativism if a God-less beginning of the universe is asserted. This will lead us to the most reasonable conclusion: only a transcendent moral Being explains our origins.

14. Beckwith and Koukl, *Relativism*, 66–67.
15. Pearcey and Thaxton, *Soul of Science*, 36.

19

Genesis, the Big Bang, and Moral Origins
The Contradictions of a God-Less View of Human Origins

Genesis as Theology

THIS CHAPTER WILL BE restricted to the moral implications of a God-less beginning, not about whether the big bang or evolution is scientific or whether the Bible opposes both. My intent is to see if the concept of a God-less big bang beginning, and the following evolutionary process, is morally consistent with how people live. If people live inconsistently with a God-less, nonmoral origin, then a God-caused beginning is more reasonable. Genesis 1 states: "In the beginning God created the heavens and the earth" (v. 1) and created humans as moral beings (v. 26). My point is this: there was a beginning, regardless of when or how it happened. More scientists are starting to affirm a cosmic beginning. But Genesis 1 is theology—a revelation of God's nature as a moral Being—not science, as seen, for example, in stars being mentioned without astronomy lessons, and plants being mentioned without biology lessons. We will see that rejecting the biblical account in Genesis 1 leaves us with no basis for *morals* as objectively real.

The Big Bang in Layman's Terms

The big bang theory is discussed by Andy Briggs in a website article. Briggs describes the big bang theory by saying that the entire energy of the universe was concentrated into one infinitely dense point; then it suddenly expanded, and this began space and time. He said that there is no evidence of a god causing this and then concludes the eighth paragraph of the article with the concession: "On the other hand, there's nothing to suggest the origin of our universe was *not* caused by a god, either."[1]

No matter how the universe began, the atheistic view is that its process has been improved by natural evolution. The atheistic view is materialistic and naturalistic. If the universe began by a sudden expansion, but God was not the cause, then matter and forces in the universe are not guided by intelligence, and morals have an impersonal origin. If God created the universe, by whatever method, and God has guided human history, then morals have a personal origin.

Genesis and the Big Bang

If Genesis 1:1 is a statement of the beginning of space and time, it is not a scientific description of God's methodology. This makes sense, since the ancient cultures would have no context for twenty-first century science. Some OT scholars say that Genesis 1:1 is not a statement of the beginning of space and time, but it is a statement of what God was going to do with the space and time that he had already created. John Goldingay says, "Genesis is not starting from the moment when nothing apart from God existed."[2]

But if Genesis 1:1 is a comment on the beginning of space and time, note two things about this verse. First, it does not claim a big bang expansion. John Walton suggests not inserting the big bang beginning into Genesis 1:1.[3] Second, it does not contradict a scientific big bang understanding either. Consider the view of Francis Collins, a Christian and a scientist, who says that Genesis 1:1 is "compatible" with science.[4]

---

1. Briggs, "What Is the Big Bang?"
2. Goldingay, *Genesis*, 27.
3. Walton, *Old Testament Theology*, 77.
4. Collins, *Language of God*, 150.

Genesis, the Big Bang, and Moral Origins

These are contrasting views. A beginning, whether by the big bang or not, was either God-caused or not. If not God-caused, then it had a mindless, purposeless, materialistic/naturalistic beginning.

In discussions with atheists, I avoid the issue of whether or not there was a big bang beginning, because such a beginning does not rule out God as the beginner anyway.

Scientism and Faith

The God-less worldview that science and reason, not faith and Scripture, give us the answers to our origins is a faith-belief system. The atheist believes, by faith, that pure reason is sufficient for answers about life. Atheism is faith-based, because there is no scientific proof that God does not exist. The secular worldview elevates science to scientism and makes this the final arbitrator of truth about reality.[5] Atheism is a philosophical position.

One morning, I told a co-worker that I had been thinking about his claim to me that faith in God made no sense. I said, "I believe by faith that God created the universe; but you believe by faith that nothing created the universe. We share the same element of faith, so why not start with God?" He put his hands in his pockets, nodded his head up and down, and said, "Something to think about." Some years later we talked, and he said that he went back to church to renew his faith in God. Maybe a simple question prompted this.

Morals and Self-Sacrifice Did Not Arrive as an Instinct

A friend proposed to me that "our moral instincts developed for our survival through evolution." I said that I had never considered this argument and would have to think about how to respond. About three months later, I told my friend I had a response, so we met for coffee.

My response was similar to the following idea. If morals are instincts from a God-less evolutionary process, then moral judgments that something ought to be done, or ought not be done, are based on human survival. Only what works towards survival is what ought to be done. There is no objective ought; just a survival ought. I told my friend that if he was right, then we should know instinctively what is best for survival. But how do we

---

5. Moreland, *Scientism and Secularism*, 26–30.

account for self-sacrifice that acts in a way opposite to the survival instinct? Why do we feel emotional when reading stories of sacrifice? Why do we feel differently from our naturalistic view? We have the theory of survival but feel at times that the opposite is true. This is inconsistent. William Lane Craig says that if a God-less survival of the fittest is correct, then we should "resist . . . self-destructive activity . . . and choose . . . our best self-interest . . . . Sacrifice for another person" does not make sense.[6]

In chapter 27 of scientist Bill Nye's book *Undeniable*,[7] Nye discusses the evolutionary purpose of self-sacrifice, sometimes called altruism—disinterested devotion to others. In summary, Nye's comment on altruism as having derived from evolution, not God, is that our instinct towards self-sacrifice is indeed for the benefit of survival, because, in the process, we help others in our community. But if so, then altruism is still through materialistic evolution, and self-sacrifice/altruism is not grounded in a universal moral mandate of what ought to be done. So why not be a suicidal terrorist, if genetic survival is not a concern for the terrorist? If the argument against suicidal terror is to say, well, it is counter-survival, then so what? The terrorist doesn't care. To resort to an evolutionary development of altruism for survival and community benefit explains nothing, because there is no universal objective basis to be altruistic. It's just my naturalistic genes; it's mere subjectivity.

If genes are predisposed towards survival instincts, then our genetic code should not move us towards self-sacrifice. It seems that we have morally schizophrenic genes. Worldview scholar Nancy Pearcey points out that some behavioral acts produce an advantage for survival, but self-sacrifice produces no advantage, so why would natural selection not have eliminated this moral notion by now?[8]

When we deny God, we have only genes left. This is not a very compelling argument for objective morals, human worth, significance, or dignity.

Molecules, Ethics, and Human Dignity

An atheist said to me during a conversation about God and morals: "Ethics are from evolution."

---

6. Craig, "Natural Theology," 75–76.
7. Nye, *Undeniable*, 207–17.
8. Pearcey, *Total Truth*, 211–16.

Genesis, the Big Bang, and Moral Origins

To respond, I said, "Let me see if I have this right. We are moral beings that developed from collisions of molecules over billions of years?"

"Yes. It's all molecules," he said.

"If everything came from colliding molecules, how could one collision be ethical and another not be? How did moral molecules arise?"

No answer was proposed for either question. I suggested that in the evolutionary process, morals must have begun at some point. This logically implies that molecules began to be ethical. How did a molecule become ethical and develop a sense of value? J. P. Moreland sums up the problem of human value and dignity if humans are merely physical objects: "If it is true that we are merely physical objects, we are of little value."[9]

John Walton states that Genesis 1 shows us that "all of the functions [light, sun, moon] are established in relation to people" and not to various gods, as in these ancient cultures; therefore, we can see that "Genesis 1 bequeaths to humanity a dignity that is not attested in the rest of the ancient Near East."[10]

The universe's beginning results from a personal Being or not. If not, our present existence would be the result of *mindlessly moving molecules* operating by naturalistic God-less laws of nature. Therefore, there is no sense that the universe has purpose for the initial creation event. But people are unable to live in an impersonal meaningless existence, so we make up a theory of altruistic genes.

Natural Molecules Cannot Have a Mind

When I think of a bowling ball, I do not have a bowling ball between my ears. The thought is not my actual brain. Neurologist Jay Lombard says that the "brain and mind are not the same."[11]

A God-less big bang beginning eliminates a divine mind behind the material universe. But how did nonconscious mindless molecules develop a rational mind following the big bang event? How would the God-less evolutionary process of colliding *mindless* molecules progress to form a brain and mind, if not infused with a purpose from a mind outside of the molecules? If the universe has no purpose, how could the brain improve and become ethical and moral?

9. Moreland, *Soul*, 15.
10. Walton, *Genesis 1*, 176–77.
11. Lombard, *Mind of God*, 11.

Journalist Tom Bethell investigated the claims of evolution given by notable scientists. Bethell notes that natural selection does not have a mind; decision making is outside of nature.[12]

Nature Is Not Personal

When denying a personal God, the only substitute is an impersonal origin of pure nature. Therefore, it follows that nature itself moved us onward. But a purely naturalistic origin, followed by chance plus time evolution, is not consistent with the human sense of dignity. To avoid despair, God-skeptics inconsistently insert some sense of personality to nature. For example, Richard Joyce speaks of nature as if it had a mind or purpose. He states that in the natural selection process, there were certain actions that "nature did not want," and he speaks of nature as if it had a "design" towards an end.[13] How did pure nature want or not want anything or formulate a design?

Neuroscientist Sam Harris suggests that evolution's natural selection process seems to "favor rampant belief formation as long as the benefits of the occasional, correct belief are great enough."[14] How could pure nature have anything that it favors?

Christians should pay attention to these kinds of statements that *borrow* biblical concepts of a personal God and then insert them into an atheistic worldview. Atheists senses a personal nature beyond the natural world but do not know where this idea comes from. Therefore, they personalize nature, because despair results if materialism is absolute.

Many atheists do believe there is a purpose and meaning to life. But why believe this? Where did this idea and feeling come from, if our origin was purely natural and materialistic? Nature is not personal.

Humans in the Image of God

The biblical description of the nature of humanity is that male and female were created in the "image" and "likeness" of God (Gen 1:26). This image and likeness implies that humans reflect back to God his moral nature, which is the source for our sense of purpose, meaning, dignity, and

---

12. Bethell, *Darwin's House of Cards*, 29.
13. Joyce, *Evolution of Morality*, 110–14.
14. S. Harris, *Moral Landscape*, 147–48.

uniqueness. A moral image cannot come from mindless molecules. In denying the image of God in humans, we lose human uniqueness. Possibly this is why some want to look, dress, and act differently. People have exchanged uniqueness for being merely different.

Physics and astronomy professors Deborah Haarsma and her husband, Loren Haarsma, state that "God did more than create our bodies. He chose to reveal himself to human beings, establishing a relationship with us beyond the relationship he has with animals.... Our significance is based on our standing in God's eyes, not on our physical size or uniqueness."[15]

God-Less Evolution Is the Perfect Argument for Racism

I was told by a woman that "life began from a lightning strike in a pool of water on a continent somewhere, and this spontaneously created a one-cell creature, and we evolved from there."

"Are you saying that all people came from this one-cell creature?" I asked.

"Yes. The cell split into two cells, and then into four, and survived to pass on its survival characteristics to other cells, and we evolved to today."

"Like in the survival of the fittest and natural selection process, you mean?"

"That's it! Inserting God isn't necessary," she proclaimed as if delivering me from a tornado of biological incompetence.

"Do you realize that you cannot live consistently with this worldview?" I calmly said.

"What do you mean?"

"You live as if your view is untrue."

"How so?" she responded.

"Why would this be a one-time-only event? Couldn't this event have happened multiple times like in ten different locations at ten different times or more?"

"I guess that's possible," she said.

I said that if her evolutionary idea is true, it opens up the multiple pools theory. If so, then couldn't one race of people assert that their original pool of water was made up of a better molecular and genetic substance than the other pool or pools, and, therefore, they were superior in quality? I suggested that her evolutionary theory is the perfect argument for racism.

---

15. Haarsma and Haarsma, *Origins*, 279.

This woman said that there is no way that racism is moral. I agreed but pointed out that her theory could not claim that racism is unjustified. She could not refute that evolution leaves open this additional theory, even though she recoiled from the implications of her evolutionary theory. She could not live consistently with the moral implications of God-less evolution from multiple pools.

We all live our lives and have a view of the dignity of humanity as if the pool of water theory is false. This should indicate to the evolutionist that a worldview of an accidental origin is faulty.

The point is, she was against racism but did not know why. We are all against racism, because we are created in the image of God and recognize every human has equal value. The God-skeptic denies the innate moral image of God in human nature but cannot live consistently without it.

Atheists Are Inconsistent in Their Evolutionary Worldview

Atheists make moral statements inconsistent with what is implied in a God-less evolutionary process. We should ask questions to draw out the inconsistency of the God-less universe theory. The following are some examples.

Endangered species should be protected. Ask: doesn't this contradict the theory of survival of the fittest? If some species are weaker, then why protect them? Isn't this just natural selection working?

Current existence comes from progressive evolution. Ask: if so, then why are there mass murderers like Hitler and Stalin? These genocidal dictators do not show humans progressing.

The fittest survive by adapting and overcoming the weak. Ask: if so, why do we commend people for self-sacrifice on behalf of the weak? Why do we love stories of people risking their life to rescue animals and people during floods in order to help them survive? How is this consistent with the theory of survival of the fittest?

Teach children ethics, so they won't act like violent animals. Ask: why are we surprised by predatory students shooting up a school when we raised children to believe they evolved from animals? Isn't opposition to these predators inconsistent with raising children to think they evolved from predators?

People are biologically determined to mistakenly believe in God. Ask: wouldn't atheists also be biologically determined to be atheists? If it is asserted that the Christian is mistaken due to genetics, then couldn't the atheist be mistaken on the same basis?

Pragmatism is the Concept of Truth via Evolution

In Cambridge, Massachusetts, in 1872, a group of scholars met and called their group the Metaphysical Club. One member was psychologist and philosopher William James. Later, James's principle of determining truth was called pragmatism, from the Greek word *pragma*, action. Pragmatism has become engrained in American culture.

James says truth is determined by "its respective practical consequences," and we discover truth by turning away from "absolutes" and towards "concreteness . . . towards facts, towards action and towards power."[16] James believed that "what makes beliefs true is not logic but results . . . in the evolving . . . of the universe."[17]

Pragmatism implies that we create truth from experience, because truth is not grounded in a transcendent God. The logical outcome is that what is morally true is determined by whether the moral principle is practical for the most people. And who determines this? Well . . . most people. But we cannot live consistently in this worldview. We are opposed to any country's worldview that their race is superior to other countries, even if most people in that country who claim superiority may believe it.

Materialism and Determinism

In some concepts of atheistic materialism, humans do not have any meaningful free will. That is, our choices are determined by our genetic make-up—hence, determinism.

G. K. Chesterton speaks of the contradiction of a deterministic worldview by stating in chapter 2 of *Orthodoxy* that, if determinism is true, fatalism results, because we would really be living in a cosmic "machine."[18]

Consider that if a deterministically produced event produces violence, how would materialistic determinism also deterministically produce

---

16. James, *Pragmatism*, 20–23.
17. Menand, *Metaphysical Club*, 220–21.
18. Chesterton, *Heretics/Orthodoxy*, 184–85.

its opposite: mercy and sacrifice? We cannot explain love by determinism, since love shows itself in sacrifice.

How would determinism produce people like inventors, artists, song writers, philosophers, and theologians, for example? Great thinkers are not in a mechanistic system; that is why they are great.

Another clear contradiction is this: if determinism is true, then the determinist is determined *to* believe it, but the nondeterminist is determined *not* to believe it. We would never know if anything we thought was true, because we might be determined to be mistaken.

Determinists live in opposition to materialistic determinism.

Why Is There Meaning Rather Than Nonsense?

"Why is there something rather than nothing?" was the first question a college philosophy professor asked a class I attended. But in a God-less universe, there is no such thing as asking *why* anything exists, since there was no mind to give *reason* to the universe. People seek truth and meaning. People do not live consistently with the concept that all is just nonsense. Meaning for life comes only from outside of the physical world.

We Are Made for Another World

Humans seem to have an affection for which atheism does not answer. Atheistic scientists explain much but inadequately explain life, because they explain only the natural world. Christianity reveals more: a sense of the realm beyond nature. Why do we have this sense? In chapter 10 of *Mere Christianity*, C. S. Lewis points out that humans exist with desires that can be satisfied within this world (babies feel hunger, which food satisfies; and ducks desire to swim, which water satisfies). Then he says, "If I find in myself a desire which no experience in this world can satisfy, the most probably explanation is that I was made for another world."[19]

---

19. Lewis, *Mere Christianity*, 136–37.

20

The Reliability of the Bible Showing Jesus as Lord

The Bible's Relevance as the Source of Spiritual Truth

The Bible Is Extraordinary Literature

THE GOSPEL STORIES ARE not what we expect. Matthew, a Jew, tells us that gentile astrologers from outside of Israel heard of Jesus's birth. But Luke, a gentile, tells us that Jewish shepherds within Israel heard of Jesus's birth. We would expect Matthew to highlight Jews, and Luke, gentiles. The Bible is literature for the imagination, even while being rationally and historically verifiable.

The Metanarrative

A narrative is a story. A metanarrative is an overarching story (from the Greek *meta*, beyond). The first section of the Bible is called the Old Testament (OT) by Christians. The *Hebrew Scriptures* is a more accurate term. The OT narrates God's work before Jesus. The next section is the New Testament (NT), which begins with Jesus and tells the story of Christianity as it moved into the late first century. The entire Bible is a metanarrative of God's work and nature.

The Bible acts as a witness to the work of Christ and is special revelation given in written form. The Bible redirects our thinking to view truth from God's perspective. Michael F. Bird says that the four Gospels in the NT "possess a theological worldview."[1]

Many people claim that there is no overarching concept of truth—no metanarrative. But this statement itself is an overarching view of truth. It claims exactly what it denies. It's like saying that my metanarrative is that there is no metanarrative.

An Authoritative Text Makes Sense

Do people need an authoritative text—a metanarrative? Yes, because we need a standard to judge between truth and error that lies outside of the realm of empirical science. We do not need the Bible to tell us the truth about a piece of granite, but we do need the Bible if we want the truth about God's nature. The Bible does not answer every conceivable intellectual question, because it is not a curiosity satisfier.

The Kinds of Text We Do Need

We need a coherent text. We do not need texts that present incoherent concepts of God. All of the biblical books show a verifiable, deliberate, and "conscious" tie to "redemptive history," but other religious writings "lack this sense of redemptive history."[2]

Therefore, we do not need mythological texts like the Hindu *Bhagavad-Gita*, which is historically unverifiable and gives us no definitive statement on the nature of God. We do not need the Quran, which does not show Allah personally interacting with humanity through his son, as in the NT narratives, because the Quran is for memorizing and reciting. We do not need the Mormon texts, which lack authority because they contradict the Bible, which came *before* the Mormon texts. We do not need Mary Baker Eddy's book, which is a physical book purporting the contradiction that the physical world is an illusion.

In contrast, we do need the Bible, which gives us a revelation of God in a form to which humans can relate. The biblical literature consists of

---

1. Bird, *Gospel of the Lord*, 229.
2. Ladd, *Theology of New Testament*, 26.

stories, poetry, allegory, parables, symbolic images, verifiable historical events, moral and theological truth, and more. This is exactly the kind of text we need.

Main Categories of Criteria Used for Biblical Reliability

Contrary to what many think, the early church did not gather and vote on which books to include into the Bible. N. T. Wright sums up the "criteria to determine the approved" collection of NT books by saying that the early church Christians looked for the following four areas of criteria:

1. If the text was written by a direct follower/apostle of Jesus or an associate
2. If the text was consistent with what the apostles of Jesus had been proclaiming
3. If the text was written close in time to Jesus and his apostles, even if an apostle did not write the text
4. If the text was accepted by a wide range of Christian church groups[3]

From another perspective, Paul Enns explains that four major tests were applied by the early church to determine which books were considered reliable and spoke with divine authority:

1. Apostolicity. The author was verified to be an apostle or connected to the apostles of Jesus.
2. Acceptance. The church at large accepted the NT books.
3. Content. The content of NT books was consistent with orthodox teaching.
4. Inspiration. The content of the NT books bore evidence of the "work of the Holy Spirit."[4]

The Bible as Objective Evidence of Christian Truth

The following are reasons to rely on the Bible as God-inspired spiritual truth.

---

3. Wright and Bird, *New Testament in Its World*, 873–74.
4. Enns, *Moody Handbook of Theology*, 174–75.

Sorting through Worldviews

No group of people could have made up the consistent Bible message over fifteen hundred years. The OT books date from 1,400 BC and were completed about 400 BC and preserved thereafter. The NT books pull hundreds of OT references into the Christian message. If all the OT books are not true, what group of people would have kept the OT books for over four hundred years just to use them to invent a NT theme of Jesus fulfilling OT Scripture? It is more likely that the consistent theme from 1,400 BC was maintained by divine inspiration.

No one in the first century would make up the Jesus of the Bible. The NT books were written by first-century Jewish followers of Jesus (except for Luke, a gentile). These writers would not have invented a Jewish messiah who claimed to be divine and expect monotheistic Jews to believe it. Nor would they invent a messiah who was solely divine, who created the universe, and expect pantheistic and polytheistic Greeks and Romans to believe it. The Jesus story would be contrary to all first-century worldviews—unlikely to have been written, unless the biblical narratives were true.

Unlikely messiah to Jews and Greeks. First-century Jews expected a messiah who would overthrow Rome and place Israel as the leading nation. Ralph Martin says that to a Jewish person, "a crucified Messiah is a contradiction in terms" and that Jesus's suffering and death would "prove that he could not be divine, since according to Greek thought, the divine cannot suffer."[5] Jewish Christians would not make up this kind of messiah.

The New Testament was universally referenced by first- and second-century Christians as a reliable source for truth. Early church theologians, such as Justin Martyr (d. 165) and Irenaeus (d. 202), made hundreds of references to Gospel texts.[6] By AD 200, Jesus's story recorded in the Gospels was well known and referenced. Craig Blomberg says that there are so many references to NT texts by early church fathers that "if the New Testament . . . were somehow lost . . . it could be reconstructed virtually in its entirety from its quotations by the church fathers."[7]

Jesus's story was written within a short period of time after his life, so if the claims were false, people would still have been alive to refute them. Consider this: Jesus was crucified about AD 30. Paul wrote 1 Corinthians about AD 55. In 1 Corinthians 15, Paul speaks of Jesus's resurrection and mentions people who witnessed Jesus alive. If Paul invented the resurrection

---

5. R. Martin, *Four Gospels*, 124.
6. McDowell, *New Evidence*, 43.
7. Blomberg and Markley, *Handbook of New Testament*, 4.

story, then there would be too many people who had been alive in AD 30 who were still alive in AD 55 to refute and discredit Paul—unless Paul was telling the truth.

A couple examples from Luke may help us with this concept.

Luke wrote the Gospel of Luke, and, later, he wrote about Paul in Acts, all before AD 66 (Paul died about AD 66, but is still alive in Acts 28). Therefore, the Gospel of Luke must have been written before AD 66. If Luke's Gospel narratives were invented, then people who had been alive in AD 30 would still have been alive around AD 66 to refute the narratives, so the Gospel of Luke would not have survived—unless it is all true.

Consider Luke 24. Luke says a known disciple named Cleopas had a personal post-resurrection encounter with Jesus, thereby making him a witness of Jesus's resurrection. Luke would not have named a specific person and the personal encounter, unless it was all true. Too many people would still have been alive in AD 66 who were alive in AD 30 to refute and discredit Luke's narrative, if Luke made it up.

These examples from Luke are too historical to be false. In other words, they are falsifiable, if false.

N. T. Wright states that the idea of a person being resurrected in the same body as he was killed in would have been rejected as a false claim, because it was outside of the Greco-Roman worldview: "Christianity was born into a world where its central claim [a bodily resurrection] was known to be false. Many believed that the dead were nonexistent; outside of Judaism, nobody believed in resurrection."[8] No one would have believed Luke or Paul's claim of a crucified and resurrected Messiah in the first century, if the claim was false.

The NT manuscript evidence shows the historical reliability of its contents. F. F. Bruce, in 1947, pointed out that over 4000 copies of early Greek manuscripts (the NT was originally written in Greek) exist in "whole or in part."[9] Neil Lightfoot, in 2003, stated that we now have "more than 5,300" NT manuscripts either in full or partial texts.[10] Regarding the record of Jesus in the Gospels, Craig Blomberg observes that the Jesus story already existed by the time Paul wrote his epistles (before AD 66), and Paul does not make any corrections of these accounts.[11]

---

8. Wright, *Resurrection of the Son*, 35.
9. Bruce, *New Testament Documents*, 16.
10. Lightfoot, *How We Got the Bible*, 34.
11. Blomberg, *Historical Reliability of Gospels*, 283–84.

The notion that the Bible has been translated so many times that our English version is unreliable is incorrect. In English Bibles, the OT is translated directly from Hebrew, and the NT is from Greek copies of the NT.[12]

The Reliability of the Resurrection Account

The following are some theories offered to refute a resurrection of Jesus's body from the dead. Comments to these theories show that these objections to Jesus's resurrection cannot possibly be true.

Jesus did not really die; he passed out. If so, we would need to believe that after Jesus endured beatings; crucifixion; and entombment without food, water, or medical treatment; then rose up days later, moved a stone from the tomb's entrance, and walked out past Roman soldiers guarding against this very event. Jesus was crucified by Roman soldiers, and they knew how to kill a man. They would not have mistaken an unconscious man for a dead one.

The disciples went to the wrong tomb, saw it was empty, and concluded Jesus had risen from the dead. Jesus was buried in a tomb owned by Joseph of Arimathea, a well-known member of the Jewish Sanhedrin council of elders in Jerusalem. All of Jesus's followers would not have mistaken a random tomb for Joseph's well-known tomb. But if they had, the enemies of Jesus would have gone to the correct tomb—Joseph's—and shown them the dead body of Jesus, thereby discrediting the resurrection claim. Christianity would have dissolved in the first century. Mark 15:47 tells us that some women saw where Jesus was laid Friday night. They would not have forgotten where this was by Sunday morning.

Jesus's dead body was stolen, so it appeared that he had risen. Matthew 27:64 states that Jesus's tomb was sealed to prevent theft. But if Jesus's body had been stolen, who stole it? If it was Jesus's enemies, then they would later have produced the body and discredited the resurrection claim. If it was Jesus's disciples, then they later suffered and died for their own false claim of a resurrection. Not likely. It is not credible to theorize that the disciples stole the body when Roman soldiers were guarding the tomb to prevent this. Actually, it was the religious leaders who paid the Roman guards to tell the story of a stolen body (Matt 28:13).

---

12. For further reading on Bible transmission, see Comfort, *Origin of the Bible*; Geisler, *Inerrancy*; Kitchen, *On Reliability of Old Testament*.

The Message of Jesus Is Relevant and Life-Changing Today

Regardless of the many anti-resurrection theories, the principle of reason remains: we have to follow the premise of any objection to see if it leads to a contradiction or to mere contrivance.

Acts 2 begins with stories taking place about fifty days after the resurrection of Jesus. After apostles spoke to people about Jesus, three thousand people responded to Christ (Acts 2:41), and shortly thereafter, the number grew to five thousand (Acts 4:4). This was not because the message was merely a new philosophical and ethical one; there was no shortage of these messages in the first century. Rather, it was people responding to the Holy Spirit confirming the resurrection story, and this is still happening today.

21

Liar, Lunatic, Legend, or Lord

Options Regarding the Nature of Jesus

Narrowing the Options to See Jesus as Lord

WE WILL CONCLUDE WITH a look at options regarding the person of Jesus Christ based on the reliability of the Bible. This process will show the biblical account as the only trustworthy witness for who Jesus really is. I owe these concluding thoughts to literary scholar C. S. Lewis's *Mere Christianity* and to authors Josh McDowell and Sean McDowell in the updated book *Evidence That Demands a Verdict*.[1]

Is Jesus a Good Moral Teacher If He Claimed Divinity?

Most non-Christians concede that Jesus was a good and wise moral teacher. If so, why follow his advice above others? Is it because Jesus is the best of them all? C. S. Lewis asks this question and concludes that we would *not* listen to Jesus if he's the best moral teacher, since humans have not listened to lesser teachers; therefore, we would not follow the advice of an advanced teacher.[2] And someone who was "merely a man and said the sort of things

---

1. McDowell and McDowell, *Evidence*, 195–204.
2. Lewis, *Mere Christianity*, 156.

Jesus said would not be a great moral teacher. He would be either a lunatic . . . a madman or something worse."[3]

Jesus did not claim to be a moral teacher. He claimed to be the divine Son of God. Note two examples of Jesus's claim of divinity for which people wanted to kill him. Jesus "was . . . making himself equal with God" (John 5:18); and those who heard him said, "You, a mere man, claim to be God" (John 10:33).

Why make these claims if they were not true, knowing the penalty for the claim was death? Josh McDowell puts the options this way: if Jesus's claims were false, they were false because Jesus knew they were false, because he was a *liar*. Or he did not know they were false, because he was a *lunatic*.[4]

Was Jesus a Liar?

If Jesus knowingly and falsely claimed to be God in order to deceive others, he cannot be considered a good moral teacher. This is cosmic identity theft. A liar is a hypocrite, which is the opposite of being good and moral.

Was Jesus a Lunatic?

Jesus could have thought he was God but was mistaken. In this case, he would be a self-deceived lunatic. But what lunatic goes about doing good works and giving the kind of wise moral teaching that Jesus set out? No one reading the Sermon on the Mount (Matt 5–7) can conclude that these are the words of a lunatic. How can we conclude that Jesus was a bad man mentally yet a good man morally? Wouldn't this kind of person be just as unreliable as a liar? Jesus was the opposite of what a lunatic is like.

But maybe the disciples were all lunatics. This is implausible, because lunatics could not have written the coherent Gospel narratives we have, nor could they have influenced the conversion of the great philosophers and teachers of the world as have come to us throughout history.

---

3. Lewis, *Mere Christianity*, 52.
4. McDowell and McDowell, *Evidence*, 197.

Was Jesus a Legend from an Invented Myth?

If Jesus was a fictional and mythical invention, then who invented him? Only his disciples would do that. But they would not invent a narrative like the Gospel stories and then subject themselves to persecution and martyrdom for their own fiction.

Jesus Is the Lord

The only conclusion is this: the written narratives about Jesus are true. This conclusion is consistent with the logical process of *sorting through worldviews*. However, becoming a Christian is not merely the result of an intellectual or logical decision. It is a moral decision. The infinite love of God is revealed to us by the Holy Spirit. The Spirit reveals our need for repentance from sin, so we repent, ask forgiveness, and invite Christ into our lives as Lord and Savior. Repentance is coming to a point of return. We do not have to morally clean ourselves up first; God does this to us afterward. Fish are cleaned, for example, after they're caught. The invitation to enjoy God's love and forgiveness is free, no matter how bad we might be.

Professor Mike McNichols writes about the various Christian views regarding the elements of the bread and wine in the Lord's Supper, also called the communion table. He insightfully concludes that the miracle is not in the physical elements at the communion event, but "the miracle" is "that any of us have been invited to the table in the first place."[5]

U2's Bono's Story

In his book, Timothy Keller gives a short excerpt of a conversation between journalist Michka Assayas and Bono, held in 2005. Bono was asked if he thought that the story of Jesus as the "Son of God" was "far-fetched." In the concluding remarks in Keller's book, Keller quotes Bono as saying, "The idea that the entire course of civilization for over half of the globe could have its fate changed and turned upside-down by a nutcase, for me that's far-fetched."[6]

---

5. McNichols, *Shadow Meal*, 125.
6. Keller, *Reason for God*, 229–30.

Consider the Options

If you are a God-skeptic, consider the options for a reasonable belief in God and Christ. Ask yourself whether any alternative makes sense and is consistent with life's experiences. You will see that Christianity is the only option, as I have attempted to show in the journey of this book.

If you aspire to know God, you must begin with Jesus Christ, which rules out any reliance on self-merit for God's favor. Jesus consumes all human efforts with love and grace. It is impossible to out-sin Jesus's desire to forgive you.

Glossary

Apologetics: To offer an answer or a defense.

Atheism: The belief that no God of any kind exists.

Atheist: A person who believes in atheism.

Beginning: An origin in time and space; opposite of infinite regression.

Contingent Existence: That which derives existence from a preceding existence; that which does not have to exist; the opposite of necessary existence.

Contradiction: A statement asserting mutually exclusive ideas making the statement impossible to be true.

Cosmology: Concepts of how the universe began and operates.

Dualism: The endless struggle between good/evil, or between a good god and an evil god.

Empirical/Empiricism: A view that truth is from verifiable scientific experiments; the opposite of metaphysics.

Hinduism: An Eastern religious belief system with the basic concept of a pantheistic worldview.

Infinite Regression: The idea of a beginning-less series of cause and effects; opposite of a beginning.

Glossary

Metanarrative: Objective statements about what is universally true.

Metaphysics: Anything beyond the physical universe; opposite of empirical/empiricism.

Necessary Existence: Uncaused existence; opposite of contingent existence.

New Age: The Hindu metaphysical worldview of the unity of the cosmos.

Ontology/Ontological: The essence, substance, or nature of something vs. being something else.

Pantheism: God and the cosmos are without distinction; God is everything.

Paradox: A thought containing concepts that may conflict but do not contradict.

Pluralism: All religious belief systems are equally valid.

Pragmatics/Pragmatism: Truth is determined by what is most practical and what works best for the most people.

Proposition: A statement that asserts a claim of what is believed to be true.

Relativism: Truth is determined by a subjective private opinion; no universal objective moral standard exists.

Self-Refuting Statement: A statement (proposition) that proves itself to be false.

Theodicy: An argument seeking to justify that the existence of God is not contradictory to the existence of evil and suffering.

Worldview: The lens through which a person interprets life; a philosophy of life.

Bibliography

Ali, Abdullah Yusuf, trans. *The Holy Quran*. Edited by Tom Griffith. Hertfordshire, UK: Wordsworth Editions Limited, 2000.
Aquinas, Thomas. *Summa Theologica*. Translated by the Fathers of the English Dominican Province. Edited by Robert Maynard Hutchins et al. Vol. 19 of *Encyclopedia Britannica*. Chicago: Encyclopedia Britannica, 1952.
Ashby, P. H. "Hinduism." In *The Perennial Dictionary of World Religions*, edited by Keith Crim et al., 306–18. San Francisco: HarperSanFrancisco, 1989.
Ayres, Lewis. "As We Are One." In *Advancing Trinitarian Theology: Explorations in Constructive Dogmatics*, edited by Oliver Crisp and Fred Sanders, 94–103. Grand Rapids: Zondervan, 2014.
Bailey, Kenneth. *Jesus through Middle Eastern Eyes: Cultural Studies in the Gospels*. Downers Grove, IL: IVP Academic, 2008.
———. *Paul through Mediterranean Eyes: Cultural Studies in 1 Corinthians*. Downers Grove, IL: IVP Academic, 2011.
Ball, Steven. "A Christian Physicist Examines the Big Bang Theory." Letourneau University, Sept. 2003. https://www.letu.edu/academics/arts-and-sciences/files/big-bang.pdf.
Barth, Karl. *Church Dogmatics*. Edited and translated by G. W. Bromiley et al. Peabody, MA: Hendrickson, 2010.
Beale, G. K. "Colossians." In *Commentary on the New Testament Use of the Old Testament*, edited by G. K. Beale and D. A. Carson. Grand Rapids: Baker Academic, 2007.
Beckwith, Francis J., and Gregory Koukl. *Relativism: Feet Firmly Planted in Mid-Air*. Grand Rapids, MI: Baker, 1998.
Beeson, Ray. *The Real Battle: Winning Daily Victories in Spiritual Warfare*. Ventura, CA: Overcomers Ministry, 2007.
Bethell, Tom. *Darwin's House of Cards: A Journalist's Odyssey through the Darwin Debates*. Seattle: Discovery Institute, 2017.
Bird, Michael. *The Gospel of the Lord: How the Early Church Wrote the Story of Jesus*. Grand Rapids: Eerdmans, 2014.

Bibliography

Birkett, K. R. "Relativism." In *New Dictionary of Christian Apologetics*, edited by W. C. Campbell-Jack et al., 604–7. Downers Grove, IL: InterVarsity, 2006.

Blomberg, Craig L. *The Historical Reliability of the Gospels*. 2nd ed. Downers Grove, IL: IVP Academic, 2007.

———, and Jennifer Foutz Markley. *A Handbook of New Testament Exegesis*. Grand Rapids: Baker Academic, 2010.

The Book of Mormon: Another Testament of Jesus Christ. Salt Lake City: Church of Jesus Christ of Latter-Day Saints, 1981.

Boyer, Steven, and Christopher Hall. *The Mystery of God: Theology for Knowing the Unknowable*. Grand Rapids: Baker Academic, 2002.

Briggs, Andy. "What Is the Big Bang?" EarthSky, June 11, 2020. https://earthsky.org/space/definition-what-is-the-big-bang.

Brown, Colin. *Miracles and the Critical Mind*. Pasadena, CA: Fuller Seminary Press, 2006.

———. *Philosophy and the Christian Faith*. Downers Grove, IL: InterVarsity, 1968.

Bruce, F. F. *The New Testament Documents: Are They Reliable?* 5th ed. Downers Grove, IL: InterVarsity, 1960.

Brunner, Emil. *Revelation and Reason*. Translated by Olive Wyon. Philadelphia: Westminster, 1946.

Brunner, Frederick Dale. *The Holy Spirit: Shy Member of the Trinity*. Eugene, OR: Wipf and Stock, 1984.

———. *A Theology of the Holy Spirit*. Grand Rapids: Eerdmans, 1970.

Campo, Juan E., and J. Gordon Melton, eds. *Encyclopedia of Islam*. New York: Checkmark, 2009.

Caner, Ergun. "Buddhism." In *The Popular Encyclopedia of Apologetics: Surveying the Evidence for the Truth of Christianity*, edited by Ed Hinson et al., 114–16. Eugene, OR: Harvest House, 2008.

Cargile, James. "Paradoxes." In *The Oxford Companion to Philosophy*, edited by Ted Honderich, 642–44. New York: Oxford University Press, 1995.

Chan, Wing-Tsit. "The Orderly Realm of Chinese Sages." In *Great Religions of the World*, edited by Merle Severy et al., 122–28. Washington, DC: National Geographic Society, 1971.

———, trans. *The Way of Lao Tzu*. New York: Bobbs-Merrill Company, 1963.

Chesterton, G. K. *Heretics/Orthodoxy*. Nashville: Thomas Nelson, 2000.

Collins, Frances. *The Language of God: A Scientist Presents Evidence for Belief*. New York: Free, 2006.

Comfort, Philip Wesley. *The Origin of the Bible*. Wheaton, IL: Tyndale House, 2003.

Copan, Paul. *True for You but Not for Me: Overcoming Objections to Christian Faith*. Minneapolis: Bethany House, 2009.

Craig, William Lane. "Cosmological Argument." In *New Dictionary of Christian Apologetics*, edited by W. C. Campbell-Jack et al., 179–82. Downers Grove, IL: InterVarsity, 2006.

———. *On Guard: Defending Your Faith with Reason and Precision*. Colorado Springs, CO: Cook, 2010.

———. "Natural Theology: Introduction." In *Philosophy of Religion: A Reader and Guide*, edited by William Lane Craig et al., 69–81. Edinburgh: Edinburgh University Press, 2002.

———. *Reasonable Faith: Christian Truth and Apologetics*. Wheaton, IL: Crossway, 2008.

Bibliography

Davis, Stephen T., and Eric T. Yang. *An Introduction to Christian Philosophical Theology: Faith Seeking Understanding*. Grand Rapids: Zondervan Academic, 2020.
Dawkins, Richard. *The God Delusion*. New York: Houghton Mifflin, 2006.
Dembski, William A. *Intelligent Design: The Bridge Between Science and Theology*. Downers Grove, IL: InterVarsity, 1999.
Eddy, Mary Baker. *Science and Health with Key to the Scriptures*. Boston: The First Church of Christ, Scientist, 1903.
Edersheim, Alfred. *The Life and Times of Jesus the Messiah*. 3rd ed. Grand Rapids: Eerdmans, 1976.
Elass, Mateen. *Understanding the Koran: A Quick Christian Guide to the Muslim Holy Book*. Grand Rapids: Zondervan, 2004.
Enns, Paul. *The Moody Handbook of Theology*. Chicago: Moody, 2008.
Epstein, Greg M. *Good without God: What a Billion Nonreligious People Do Believe*. New York: HarperCollins, 2010.
Esposito, John L. *The Oxford Dictionary of Islam*. New York: Oxford University Press, 2003.
Fairweather, Jack. *The Volunteer: One Man, an Underground Army, and the Secret Mission to Destroy Auschwitz*. New York: HarperCollins, 2019.
Feser, Edward. *Five Proofs of the Existence of God*. San Francisco: Ignatius, 2017.
Fraser, Caroline. *God's Perfect Child: Living and Dying in the Christian Science Church*. New York: Picador, 1999.
Freedman, David Noel, et al., eds. *Eerdmans Dictionary of the Bible*. Grand Rapids: Eerdmans, 2000.
Fuchida, Mitsuo. *For That One Day: Memoirs of Mitsuo Fuchida, Commander of the Attack on Pearl Harbor*. Translated by Douglas T. Shinsato and Tadanori Urabe. Kamuela, HI: eXperience, 2011.
Galfard, Christophe. *The Universe in Your Hand: A Journey through Space, Time, and Beyond*. New York: Flatiron, 2015.
Gard, Richard, ed. *Buddhism*. New York: Braziller, 1961.
Geisler, Norman. *Baker Encyclopedia of Christian Apologetics*. Grand Rapids: Baker, 1999.
———. *If God, Why Evil?* Minneapolis: Bethany House, 2011.
———. *Inerrancy*. Grand Rapids: Zondervan, 1980.
———, and Abdul Saleeb. *Answering Islam: The Crescent in Light of the Cross*. Grand Rapids: Baker, 2002.
Geivett, R. Douglas. "The Kalaam Cosmological Argument." In *To Everyone an Answer: A Case for the Christian Worldview*, edited by Francis J. Beckwith et al., 61–76. Downers Grove, IL: IVP Academic, 2004.
Goldingay, John. *Genesis*. Baker Commentary on the Old Testament. Grand Rapids: Baker Academic, 2020.
———. *Israel's Faith*. Vol. 2 of *Old Testament Theology*. Downers Grove, IL: IVP Academic, 2006.
———. *Israel's Gospel*. Vol. 1 of *Old Testament Theology*. Downers Grove, IL: IVP Academic, 2003.
Grenz, Stanley. *Theology for the Community of God*. Grand Rapids: Eerdmans, 1994.
Groothuis, Douglas. *Christian Apologetics: A Comprehensive Case for Biblical Faith*. Downers Grove, IL: IVP Academic, 2011.
Guinness, Os. "Time For Truth." In *A Place for Truth: Leading Thinkers Explore Life's Hardest Questions*, edited by Dallas Willard, 37–54. Downers Grove, IL: InterVarsity, 2010.

Bibliography

Haarsma, Deborah, and Loren D. Haarsma. *Origins: Christian Perspectives on Creation, Evolution, and Intelligent Design*. Grand Rapids: Faith Alive, 2011.

Hackett, Stuart. *The Recovery of the Highest Good: A Philosophical and Critical Ethic*. Eugene, OR: Wipf and Stock, 2009.

———. *The Resurrection of Theism*. Chicago: Moody, 1957.

Hamlyn, D. W. "Empiricism." In *The Encyclopedia of Philosophy*. Edited by Paul Edwards et al., 2:499–505. New York: MacMillian, 1967.

Harris, Dana M. "Messianic Expectations in Jesus's Day." In *The Baker Illustrated Bible Background Commentary*, edited by J. Scott Duval and J. Daniel Hays, 758–60. Grand Rapids: Baker, 2020.

Harris, Sam. *The Moral Landscape: How Science Can Determine Human Values*. New York: Free, 2010.

Hasker, William. *The Triumph of God over Evil: Theodicy for a World of Suffering*. Downers Grove, IL: IVP Academic, 2008.

Hawking, Stephen. *A Brief History of Time: From the Big Bang to Black Holes*. New York: Bantam, 1988.

———, and Leonard Mlodinow. *The Grand Design*. New York: Bantam, 2010.

Henry, Jerry M. "Trinity." In *Holman Illustrated Bible Dictionary*, edited by Chad Brand et al., 1625–27. Nashville: Holman Bible, 2003.

Hill, Jonathan. *The History of Christian Thought*. Downers Grove, IL: InterVarsity, 2003.

Hirsch, Ammiel, and Josef Reinman. *One People, Two Worlds: A Reform Rabbi and an Orthodox Rabbi Explore the Issues That Divide Them*. New York: Schocken, 2002.

Insight on the Scriptures. Vol. 2. Brooklyn, NY: Watch Tower Bible and Tract Society, 1988.

James, William. *Pragmatism*. New York: Barnes and Nobel, 2003.

Joktan, Ahmed. *From Mecca to Christ: A True Story from the Son of the Meccan Mufti*. Wenatchee, WA: Proclaim, 2020.

Jones, Clay. *Why Does God Allow Evil? Compelling Answers for Life's Toughest Questions*. Eugene, OR: Harvest House, 2017.

Joyce, Richard. *The Evolution of Morality*. Cambridge, MA: MIT Press, 2006.

Kant, Immanuel. *The One Possible Basis for a Demonstration of the Existence of God*. Translated by Gordon Treash. Lincoln: University of Nebraska Press, 1979.

Kateregga, Badru D., and David W. Shenk. *A Muslim and a Christian in Dialogue*. Scottdale, PA: Herald, 1997.

Keller, Timothy. *The Reason for God: Belief in an Age of Skepticism*. New York: Dutton, 2008.

———. *Walking with God through Pain and Suffering*. New York: Dutton, 2013.

Kessler, Gary. *Voices of Wisdom: Multicultural Philosophy*. Belmont, CA: Wadsworth Group, 2003.

Kitchen, K. A. *On the Reliability of the Old Testament*. Grand Rapids: Eerdmans, 2003.

Kittle, Gerhard, and Gerhard Friedrich, eds. *Theological Dictionary of the New Testament*. Translated by Geoffrey Bromiley. Grand Rapids: Eerdmans, 1964–1976.

Koukl, Gregory. *The Story of Reality: How the World Began, How it Ends, and Everything Important in Between*. Grand Rapids: Zondervan, 2017.

———. *Tactics: A Game Plan for Discussing your Christian Convictions*. Grand Rapids: Zondervan, 2009.

———. "Tactics: Applying Apologetics to Everyday Life." In *To Everyone an Answer: A Case for the Christian Worldview*, edited by Francis Beckwith et al., 47–56. Downers Grove, IL: IVP Academic, 2004.

Bibliography

Kreeft, Peter. *Socratic Logic*. South Bend, IN: St. Augustine's, 2010.

———. *Summa Philosophica*. South Bend, IN: St. Augustine's, 2012.

———, and Ronald K. Tacelli. *Handbook of Christian Apologetics*. Downers Grove, IL: InterVarsity, 1994.

Küng, Hans. *Islam: Past, Present and Future*. Translated by John Bowden. Oxford, UK: Oneworld, 2007.

Kyokai, Bukkyo Dendo. *The Teaching of Buddha*. Tokyo: Kosaido, 1966.

Lacey, Alan. "Empiricism." In *Philosophy: The Oxford Guide*, edited by Ted Honderich, 242–45. New York: Oxford University Press, 2005.

Ladd, George Eldon. *A Theology of the New Testament*. Grand Rapids: Eerdmans, 1993.

Lawrence, B. "Muslim." In *The Perennial Dictionary of World Religions*, edited by Keith Crim et al., 508. San Francisco: HarperSanFrancisco, 1989.

Lee, Siu-Fan. *Logic: A Complete Introduction*. London: Carmelite House, 2017.

Lennox, John C. *Can Science Explain Everything?* Epson, UK: Good Book Company, 2019.

Letham, Robert. *The Holy Trinity: In Scripture, History, Theology, and Worship*. Phillipsburg, NJ: P&R, 2019.

Lewis, C. S. *God in the Dock: Essays on Theology and Ethics*. Grand Rapids: Eerdmans, 1970.

———. *Mere Christianity*. New York: HarperCollins, 2001.

———. *Miracles*. New York: HarperOne, 1947.

Lightfoot, Neil R. *How We Got the Bible*. 3rd ed. Grand Rapids: Baker, 2003.

Lombard, Jay. *The Mind of God: Neuroscience, Faith, and a Search for the Soul*. New York: Harmony, 2017.

"Trinity." In *The Baker Illustrated Bible Dictionary*, edited by Tremper Longman III et al., 1667–70. Grand Rapids: Baker, 2013.

Love, Rick. *Peace Catalysts: Resolving Conflict in Our Families, Organizations and Communities*. Downers Grove, IL: InterVarsity, 2014.

Lowe, E. J. "Ontology." In *The Oxford Companion to Philosophy*, edited by Ted Honderich, 634–35. New York: Oxford University Press, 1995.

Markos, Louis. *Apologetics for the Twenty-First Century*. Wheaton, IL: Crossway, 2010.

Martin, Michael. *Atheism: A Philosophical Justification*. Philadelphia: Temple University Press, 1990.

Martin, Ralph P. *The Four Gospels*. New Testament Foundations: A Guide for Christian Students 1. Eugene, OR: Wipf and Stock, 1994.

Mautner, Thomas. *Dictionary of Philosophy*. 2nd ed. London: Penguin, 2010.

McConkie, Bruce. *Mormon Doctrine*. 2nd ed. Salt Lake City: Bookcraft, 1966.

McDowell, Josh. *The New Evidence That Demands a Verdict*. Nashville: Nelson, 1999.

———, and Sean McDowell. *Evidence That Demands a Verdict: Life-Changing Truth for a Skeptical World*. Nashville: Thomas Nelson, 2017.

McKeever, Bill, and Eric Johnson. *Mormonism 101: Examining the Religion of the Latter-Day Saints*. Grand Rapids: Baker, 2000.

McNichols, Michael. *Shadow Meal: Reflections on the Eucharist*. Eugene, OR: Wipf and Stock, 2010.

Mehrotra, Rajoiv, ed. *The Essential Dalai Lama: His Important Teachings*. New York: Penguin, 2005.

Menand, Louis. *The Metaphysical Club*. New York: Farrar, Straus and Giroux, 2001.

Millet, Robert L., and Gregory C. V. Johnson. *Bridging the Divide: The Continuing Conversation Between a Mormon and an Evangelical*. Rhinebeck, NY: Monkfish, 2009.

Bibliography

Moreland, J. P. "Arguments for the Existence of God." In Certificate of Achievement in Christian Apologetics, Module 1. La Mirada, CA: Biola University, 2019.

———. *Scientism and Secularism: Learning to Respond to a Dangerous Ideology.* Wheaton, IL: Crossway, 2018.

———. *The Soul: How We Know It's Real and Why It Matters.* Chicago: Moody, 2014.

———. "Why Science Needs Philosophy." In *Theistic Evolution: A Scientific, Philosophical, and Theological Critique*, edited by J. P. Moreland et al., 547–59. Wheaton, IL: Crossway, 2017.

———, and William Lane Craig. *Philosophical Foundations for a Christian Worldview.* Downers Grove, IL: InterVarsity, 2003.

Mouw, Richard J. *Talking with Mormons: An Invitation to Evangelicals.* Grand Rapids: Eerdmans, 2012.

Nash, Ronald H. "The Problem of Evil." In *To Everyone an Answer: A Case for the Christian Worldview*, edited by Francis Beckwith et al., 203–23. Downers Grove, IL: IVP Academic, 2004.

Nye, Bill. *Undeniable: Evolution and the Science of Creation.* Edited by Corey S. Powell. New York: St. Martin's Griffin, 2015.

Oliphint, K. Scott. *Reasons for Faith: Philosophy in the Service of Theology.* Phillipsburg, NJ: P&R, 2006.

Olson, Roger. *The Mosaic of Christian Belief: Twenty Centuries of Unity and Diversity.* 2nd ed. Downers Grove, IL: IVP Academic, 2016.

Organ, Troy Wilson. *Hinduism: Its Historical Development.* Woodbury, NY: Barron's Educational Series, 1974.

Overman, Dean L. *A Case for the Divinity of Jesus: Examining the Earliest Evidence.* Lanham, MD: Rowman and Littlefield, 2010.

———. *A Case for the Existence of God.* Lanham, MD: Rowman and Littlefield, 2009.

Pao, David W. *Colossians and Philemon.* Edited by Clinton E. Arnold et al. Exegetical Commentary on the New Testament. Grand Rapids: Zondervan, 2012.

Pearcey, Nancy. *Total Truth: Liberating Christianity from Its Cultural Captivity.* Wheaton, IL: Crossway, 2005.

———, and Charles B. Thaxton. *The Soul of Science: Christian Faith and Natural Philosophy.* Wheaton, IL: Crossway, 1994.

Peterman, Gerald, and Andrew Schmutzer. *Between Pain and Grace: A Biblical Theology of Suffering.* Chicago: Moody, 2016.

Plantinga, Alvin. *God, Freedom, and Evil.* Grand Rapids: Eerdmans, 1974.

Pratt, Douglas. "Religious Pluralism and Dialogue." In *Theological Issues in Christian-Muslim Dialogue*, edited by Charles Tieszen, 112–24. Eugene, OR: Pickwick, 2018.

Quinn, Philip L. "Pantheism." In *Philosophy: The Oxford Guide*, edited by Ted Honderich, 677. New York: Oxford University Press, 2005.

Ramadan, Teriq. "Muslims, Prophethood, and Jesus." In *Theological Issues in Christian-Muslim Dialogue*, edited by Charles Teiszen, 42–52. Eugene, OR: Pickwick, 2018.

Reese, William. *Dictionary of Philosophy and Religion: Eastern and Western Thought.* Expanded ed. Amherst, NY: Humanity, 1996.

Robinson, Stephen E., and Craig L. Blomberg. *How Wide the Divide: A Mormon and an Evangelical in Conversation.* Downers Grove, IL: InterVarsity, 1997.

Ross, Hugh. *The Creator and the Cosmos.* 3rd ed. Colorado Springs, CO: NavPress, 2001.

Russell, Jeffrey Burton. *Exposing Myths about Christianity: A Guide to Answering 145 Viral Lies and Legends.* Grand Rapids: IVP Books, 2012.

Bibliography

Saddhatissa, H. *The Buddha's Way*. New York: George Braziller, 1971.
Sanders, Fred. "What Trinitarian Theology Is For." In *Advancing Trinitarian Theology: Explorations in Constructive Dogmatics*, edited by Oliver Crisp and Fred Sanders, 21–41. Grand Rapids: Zondervan, 2014.
Schreiner, Thomas. *Romans: Baker Exegetical Commentary on the New Testament*. Grand Rapids: Baker Academic, 1998.
Schroeder, Gerald. *The Science of God: The Convergence of Scientific and Biblical Wisdom*. New York: Free, 1997.
Schuhmacher, Stephan et al., eds. *The Encyclopedia of Eastern Philosophy and Religion: Buddhism, Taoism, Zen, Hinduism*. Translated by Michael Kohn et al. Boston: Shambhala, 1986.
Shelley, Bruce. *Church History in Plain Language*. Nashville: Nelson, 1995.
Smart, J. J. C. "The Province of Philosophy." In *Introduction to Philosophy: Classical and Contemporary Reading*, edited by John Perry and Michael Bratman, 12–20. 3rd ed. New York: Oxford University Press, 1999.
Smith, George Albert. *Doctrine and Covenants; The Pearl of Great Price*. Salt Lake City: Deseret, 1973. Two books in one vol.
Smith, George H. *Atheism: The Case against God*. Amherst, NY: Prometheus, 1989.
Smith, Joseph Fielding, ed. *Teachings of the Prophet Joseph Smith*. Salt Lake City: Deseret, 1976.
Stackhouse, John G., Jr. *Can God Be Trusted? Faith and the Challenge of Evil*. Downers Grove, IL: InterVarsity, 2009.
Stenger, Victor J. *God: The Failed Hypothesis; How Science Shows That God Does Not Exist*. Amherst, NY: Prometheus, 2007.
Suzuki, D. T. *An Introduction to Zen Buddhism*. New York: Grove, 1964.
Talmage, James. *The Articles of Faith*. Salt Lake City: Church of Jesus Christ of Latter-Day Saints, 1973.
Torrance, Thomas F. *The Christian Doctrine of God: One Being, Three Persons*. Edinburgh: T&T Clark, 1996.
Tour, James W. "The Mystery of the Origin of Life." Lecture on YouTube, March 18, 2019. https://www.youtube.com/watch?v=zU7Lww-sBPg.
Towler, Solala. *The Tao of Intimacy and Ecstasy: Realizing the Promise of Spiritual Union*. Boulder, CO: Sounds True, 2014.
Townsend, Tim. *Mission at Nuremberg: An American Army Chaplain and the Trial of the Nazis*. New York: HarperCollins, 2014.
Turek, Frank. *Stealing from God: Why Atheists Need God to Make Their Case*. Colorado Springs, CO: NavPress, 2014.
———, and Norman Geisler. *I Don't Have Enough Faith to Be an Atheist*. Wheaton, IL: Crossway, 2004.
Waltke, Bruce K. *An Old Testament Theology: An Exegetical, Canonical, and Thematic Approach*. Grand Rapids: Zondervan, 2007.
Walton, John. *Genesis 1 as Ancient Cosmology*. Winona Lake, IN: Eisenbrauns, 2011.
———. *Old Testament Theology for Christians: From Ancient Context to Enduring Belief*. Grand Rapids: InterVarsity, 2017.
———, and Craig Keener. *NIV Cultural Backgrounds Study Bible: Bringing to Life the Ancient World of Scripture*. Grand Rapids, MI: Zondervan, 2016.
Weber, Otto. *Foundations of Dogmatics*. Translated by Darrell Guder. Vol. 1. Grand Rapids: Eerdmans, 1981.

Bibliography

Webster's New World: Roget's A–Z Thesaurus. Cleveland: Wiley, 1999.

Wiesenthal, Simon. *The Sunflower: On the Possibilities and Limits of Forgiveness*. New York: Schocken, 1997.

Wilson, Mark. "Revelation." In *The Baker Illustrated Bible Background Commentary*, edited by J. Scott Duvall and J. Daniel Hays, 1299–338. Grand Rapids: Baker, 2020.

Wood, W. Jay. *Epistemology: Becoming Intellectually Virtuous*. Downers Grove, IL: InterVarsity, 1998.

Wright, N. T. *Evil and the Justice of God*. Downers Grove, IL: InterVarsity, 2006.

———. *The New Testament and the People of God*. Minneapolis: Fortress, 1992.

———. *The Resurrection of the Son of God*. Minneapolis: Fortress, 2003.

———, and Michael F. Bird. *The New Testament in Its World: An Introduction to the History, Literature, and Theology of the First Christians*. Grand Rapids: Zondervan Academic, 2019.

Zaka, Anees. "Here I Stand: An Historical, Biblical, & Missiological View of Islam." In *A Christian Worldview: Essays from a Reformed Perspective*, edited by C. N. Willborn, 59–73. Taylors, SC: Presbyterian Press, 2008.

www.ingramcontent.com/pod-product-compliance
Lightning Source LLC
Chambersburg PA
CBHW071453150426
43191CB00008B/1336